RELAX WITH A SMILE

Better is he who shows a smiling countenance than he who offers milk to drink.

THE TALMUD

*

SMILE: a curve that sets most things straight.

Anon

*

Prithee, don't look with that violent and inflexible wise face, like *Solomon* at the dividing of the child in an old tapestry hanging.

WILLIAM CONGREVE

*

By necessity, by proclivity—and by delight, we all quote.

T. W. EMERSON

COMPILED BY C. KENT WRIGHT

RELAX
WITH
A SMILE

An Anthology Designed Mainly for After-Dinner Speakers

WITH A FOREWORD

BY

THE RT. HON. LORD BIRKETT, P.C., LL.D.

LONDON: GEORGE ALLEN & UNWIN LTD

FIRST PUBLISHED IN 1960

PRINTED IN GREAT BRITAIN
in 10pt Pilgrim type
BY THE EAST MIDLAND PRINTING CO LTD
BURY ST EDMUNDS, SUFFOLK

I DEDICATE THIS ANTHOLOGY,
IN GENERAL, TO ALL

gay, witty, frolicsome, cheerful, spruce, jocund, handsome, witty, courteous, gentle blades, and delicious, charming, mirthful, lovely, magnetic, sprightly, ripe, young, choice, dear, alluring, capricious, clever, sweet and ravishing ladies.

AND, IN PARTICULAR, TO
LISA, MARTIN AND THE TWINS

19th February 1960

TO THE READER

Faultes escaped in the Printing, correcte with your pennes;
omitted by my negligence, overslippe with your patience:
committed by ignorance, remit with favour.

LYLY, *Euphues and his England*

Mr Kent Wright has invited me to write a short Foreword to his Anthology and I willingly do so.

After-dinner speaking has long been recognized as part of our way of life and it is well that those who indulge in it should be encouraged and assisted by those who know the pains and the pleasures of it, and can point out some of the pitfalls which beset the inexperienced. Mr Kent Wright provides some amusing material for speeches and sound advice for speakers. The material should be used sparingly but the advice should be followed thankfully.

It is frequently said that in our day oratory of any kind has fallen into disuse and that men and women are no longer interested in public speaking. I am quite sure from my own experience that this is not true; but in the swiftly-moving age in which we live men can no longer devote the time to preparation that was given to it in the days when the world was very much different. The noblest short speech that ever came from the lips of man was perhaps Abraham Lincoln's speech at Gettysburg. Ten sentences were spoken in five minutes and they will live so long as language endures. But every word of that speech had been carefully written out long before the time of its delivery and the documents in the Library of Congress bear witness to the immense pains taken by Lincoln in preparing for the great occasion. The truth is that every worthwhile speech demands preparation and is little good without it. The late Lord Hewart (a Prince of after-dinner speaking in his day) used to say that the speech which sounded so spontaneous because of the ease and readiness of the delivery, and which was given without a note, had probably kept the speaker awake for many a long night in the mental throes of preparation.

Prepare carefully and rehearse the speech is the best

advice of all. Follow the directions of Mr Kent Wright and weave your pattern of grave and gay; use humour judiciously; remember the vast importance of brevity; never tell a doubtful story and avoid offending any of your hearers. When you do speak be sure you speak so that you can be heard. Try and emulate Francis Bacon of whom Ben Jonson said : 'His hearers could not cough or look aside from him without loss.'

And whatever else you do *make sure that you use good English*. The hall-mark of a first-class speech is style, and Swift's famous phrase is still true : that 'proper words in proper places make the true definition of a style.' The right choice of words from our marvellous English tongue can give infinite pleasure to the hearers and sometimes almost achieve enchantment.

My Lords, Ladies and Gentlemen, I give you the toast of the after-dinner speaker coupled with the name of Mr Kent Wright.

BIRKETT

Unlike poets, after-dinner speakers are made, not born. By the careful preparation of speeches and practice in delivering them a man may amuse and entertain his well-fed audience who may have assembled on a great variety of occasions. With friends, said Francis Bacon, a man *tosseth* his thoughts. Those who have just consumed a good dinner, whether they are personal friends of the speaker or not, are in a friendly mood, and so are in a receptive and benignant state of mind, ready to catch the thoughts when tossed. But the speech which sounds effortless and unprepared is usually, in reality, a 'carefully prepared impromptu'.

In England speaking after dinner has almost attained the popularity of a national sport. We seldom lose an opportunity for holding a dinner to celebrate *something*.

Speeches may range in importance from the Prime Minister's speech at the annual dinner of the Lord Mayor of London or of the Royal Academy to the speech of the president of a local farmers' union or of any local sporting club or association. It is because of the great variety of subjects with which an after-dinner speaker may be called upon to deal that I have made this motley collection of epigrams, witticisms, anecdotes and stories from many sources—from the 'classics', and modern authors, as well as from the more ephemeral literature in magazines and newspapers. I might claim with Juvenal that 'Quidquid agunt homines del, . . . nostri farrago libelli est'.

Why, it may be asked, is a section on the weather included in an anthology designed primarily for after-dinner speakers? May it not be useful, I reply, for the annual dinner of the Society of Meteorologists, or, if there is no such society, to scores of gardeners' or farmers' associations?

In other sections will be found material which may be

used both for and against husbands and wives, doctors, lawyers, dons, painters, politicians, scientists, preachers, motorists, civil servants, journalists and of course on 'the ladies'. There are, too, sections devoted to subjects of such perennial interest as cats, dogs, horses, money, marriage, children, food, sport, politics and conversation. Sometimes, esconced between two witticisms, you may find some serious thought or reflection—seriousness *will* break in sometimes, as Dr Johnson's unphilosophic friend did *not* say.

About how to weave the aphorisms or witticisms into the texture of your speech I will not offer any advice. All that I will venture to say about the functions of a speech is:

(1) It should express, sincerely and in a pleasantly informal way, whatever may be the theme of the toast or reply—good wishes to an individual, the prosperity of a business, or the health of 'the ladies'.

(2) It should both amuse and interest the audience.

It follows that a good after-dinner speech should be a mixture of the grave and the gay. Some speakers prefer to start with a joke and end on a serious note, others *vice versa*. The late Stephen Leacock once wrote: 'It is now a convention that all speakers at banquets must begin with a funny story. I am quite sure that if the Archbishop of Canterbury were invited to address the Episcopal Church of America, the senior bishop would introduce him with a story of an old donkey, and the Archbishop would rise to reply with a story about a commercial traveller.'

Be that as it may, the joke, the epigram, the pun and the paradox may all (though preferably not all together) supply useful ingredients for this special form of oratory, while the great virtue of the aphorism is, as Dr Johnson said, 'the comprehension of some obvious and useful truth in a few words'. Aim at a judicious mixture of the serious and the flippant; and do not *overload* your speech with anecdotes, wisecracks or witticisms. One of each, if it is relevant and adroitly introduced, will go quite a long way in an after-dinner speech. Let a reasonable brevity be the keynote of your after-dinner speeches! A good maxim to follow is: 'Never speak for so long that your audience cannot remember the beginning of your speech'. It is much better to leave your audience longing for more, than to be like the long-winded parson in the story.

'Has he finished yet?' whispered a rather deaf member of the congregation to his neighbour.

'Aye, he finished five minutes ago,' the neighbour replied, 'but he doesn't know when to gi' ower.'

I have included one or two 'chestnuts'—but I think that they are good ones. Also, I have often deliberately placed expressions of opinion, which are wildly inconsistent, in close proximity to each other. This has been done on the 'Will the Brains Trust please reconcile these statements' principle.

Sir James Barrie professed to think speech-making 'the lowest of the arts—little more than a knack', and considered its exercise 'rather a degradation'. He took pains, however, to be degraded gracefully, and for my part I profoundly disagree with his professed opinion. I believe that the art of speech-making should rank high among the arts, and that to excel in it is one of the attributes of a truly civilized man or woman.

I should like to record my profound indebtedness to Lord Birkett, who excels in *every* kind of oratory, for having written such an admirable Foreword to my anthology.

In conclusion, may I express the hope that my anthology will not only assist after-dinner speakers to amuse and entertain their fellow-guests, but that it may amuse some readers who have never made, and never *intend* to make an after-dinner speech. Sink comfortably into your arm-chairs, my little ones, light your pipes, open a page at random—and relax with a smile!

C.K.W.

CONTENTS

ADVERTISING

*

You can tell the ideals of a nation by its advertisements.
NORMAN DOUGLAS

When you have a public that is literate without being discriminating, they are bound hand and foot.
DAVID DACHES

Advertising Agency: eighty-five per cent confusion and fifteen per cent commission.
FRED ALLEN

I do not read advertisements—I would spend all my time wanting things.
THE ARCHBISHOP OF CANTERBURY

AGE

*

There is more felicity on the far side of baldness than young men can possibly imagine.

LOGAN PEARSALL SMITH

I have never known a person to live to 110, or more, and then die to be remarkable for anything else.

JOSH BILLINGS

To me, old age is always fifteen years older than I am.

BERNARD BARUCH

Goethe, he mused, was older than me when he was writing love poems to young girls. Renoir at eighty-six . . . Titian, Voltaire, Verdi, composed *Falstaff* at eighty. But artists are perhaps exceptions.

MURIEL SPARK

As soon as a man acquires fairly good sense, it is said that he is an old fogey.

E. W. HOWE

To be seventy years young is sometimes far more cheerful and hopeful than to be forty years old.

OLIVER WENDELL HOLMES

Childhood itself is scarcely more lovely than a cheerful, kindly, sunshiny old age.

L. M. CHILD

No wise man ever wished to be younger.

DEAN SWIFT

'Sir,' said Dr. Johnson, 'I love the acquaintance of young people; because, in the first place, I don't like to think my-

16

self growing old. In the next place, young acquaintances must last the longest, if they do last.'

JAMES BOSWELL

The first forty years of life give us the text; the next thirty supply the commentary.   SCHOPENHAUER

A teenager was complaining about the modern boy. 'As soon,' she said, 'as they get old enough to stop acting silly, they get interested in science fiction.'

*   *   *

When a woman tells you her age, it's all right to look surprised, but don't scowl.   WILSON MIZNER

If youth is a fault, one soon gets rid of it.

GOETHE

The Golden Age is golden only in retrospect, and merely gilded upon examination.

PROFESSOR E. W. F. TOMLIN

Every age is fed on illusions, lest men should renounce life early and the human race come to an end.

JOSEPH CONRAD

As soon as people are old enough to know better, they don't know anything at all.   OSCAR WILDE

Thirty-five is a very attractive age; London society is full of women who have of their own free choice remained thirty-five for years.   OSCAR WILDE

Only the young die good.   OLIVER HERFORD

Beware of what you wish for in youth, for in middle age you will surely achieve it.   GOETHE

The first hundred years are the hardest.

WILSON MIZNER

'It seems but yesterday,' he would say, 'that I was as young as you are. We imagine that we can turn the pages slowly, one by one, pausing at each paragraph. But it is not like that, believe me. The pages are caught by a gust of wind, a hurricane, and they flutter and rush through our fingers.'   SIR HAROLD NICOLSON

The beauty of being young is that so many things have, delusively, a personal reference to you; only to age is it plain that things matter and you don't.

LORD VANSITTART

Before my (eightieth) birthday I looked on myself as a youngish seventy; on November 19th I woke up at least eighty-five. Desmond MacCarthy used to say that people didn't get gradually older, but now and then fell off a ledge, and this was what happened to me.

SIR EDWARD MARSH
(in a letter)

I think myself as vigorous as ever in the faculties of my soul, excepting only my memory, which is not impaired to any great degree; and if I lose not more of it, I have no great reason to complain. What judgment I had, increases rather than diminishes; and thoughts, such as they are, come crowding in so fast upon me, that my only difficulty is to chuse or reject.   JOHN DRYDEN (aetat. 68)

"There aren't as many owd folk about as there used to be," Ben said to his wife as she cleared the table. He took the cover to the door to shake. There was a sudden scurry as a gang of youngsters who had been playing outside, bolted.

'Hey up,' hissed one. 'Th'owd lad's here.'

Ben retired indoors, a sadder and wiser man.

'I know now where th'owd folk are,' he told his wife. 'We're 'em.'   THE DALESMAN

AMERICANS

*

Most Americans are born drunk. . . . They have a sort or permanent intoxication from within, a sort of invisible champagne.   G. K. CHESTERTON

As no man is so dreadfully well-dressed as a well-dressed American, so no man is so terribly well-mannered as a well-mannered American.

*   *   *

'We ain't got hold of culture yet, but when we do get her, boy, we'll make her hum."
(Saying which New Yorkers used to ascribe to the inhabitants of Chicago.)

ANIMALS

*

Of all God's creatures there is only one that cannot be made the slave of the lash. That one is the cat. If man could be crossed with the cat, it would improve man, but it would deteriorate the cat.   MARK TWAIN

When I play with my cat, who knows but that she regards me more of a plaything than I do her?
                                                                                              MONTAIGNE

Cat: A pygmy lion who loves mice, hates dogs, and patronises human beings.   OLIVER HERFORD

> Dogs look up at you;
> Cats look down on you
> But a pig's your equal.
>   COUNTRY SAYING

A dog teaches a boy fidelity, perseverance, and to turn around three times before lying down.
                                                                                    ROBERT BENCHLEY

To the dog every man is Napoleon, hence the constant popularity of dogs.   ALDOUS HUXLEY

The great pleasure of a dog is that you may make a fool of yourself with him and not only will he not scold you, but he will make a fool of himself too.
                                                                                      SAMUEL BUTLER

Man is a dog's ideal of what God should be.
                                                                                    HOLBROOK JACKSON

A man met a friend who was leading a very thin-looking dog. The following conversation ensued:

'Are you going to the show?'

'Sure, I am.'

'Are you going to take that dog?'

'Oh, yes, I am going to take the dog.'

BARK: This is a sound made by dogs when excited. Dogs bark at milkmen, postmen, yourself, visitors to the house and other dogs: some of them bark at nothing. For some reason dogs tend not to bark at burglars, bailiffs and income tax collectors, at whom they wag their tails in the most friendly manner.   GEOFFREY WILLIAMS

An Englishman was trying to persuade a Chinaman to enter a house at the front door of which a large dog was barking loudly.

'Come on,' he said, 'you know the proverb "A barking dog never bites," '

'Yes,' said the Chinaman dubiously, 'I know proverb; you know proverb; but does *dog* know proverb?"

*   *   *

'You don't mean you are going to exhibit the dog?'

'Yes, I do.'

'But you don't expect him to take a prize.'

'No, I don't expect him to take a prize, but he's going to meet an awful lot of nice dogs.'

*   *   *

When a man wants to murder a tiger he calls it sport, when a tiger wants to murder him he calls it ferocity.
          GEORGE BERNARD SHAW

A sporting host who was unable to go out, armed a guest with a gun and a bag of ferrets.

The guest came back smiling.

'Grand sport,' he said. 'Have you any more of those squirrel things? I've shot the lot you gave me.''

The Dalesman

Many years ago at a North Country horse fair I heard a dealer wax enthusiastic over the intelligence of a horse he wanted to sell.

'That there 'orse,' he said, 'wants treating very gentle, because he's that artful. Why, if any silly bloke was to go and ill-treat him, that there 'orse would bear malice just like a Christian!'

The Dalesman

A horse is entitled to as much consideration as a human being—often more.

HIS HONOUR J. TUDOR REES

I was invariably dragged round the stables before or after lunch to see the hunters. Every horse looked exactly alike to me, and I was always completely at a loss for the correct comment to make on these occasions. 'What nice paws it's got,' for instance, I found never went down, and after a very short time, I gave up trying.

SIR CHRISTOPHER LYNCH-ROBINSON

'Are you concerned with the promotion of goodwill among sheep?—A sort of "lonely ewes" club?'

Question in 'What's My Line?'

Sir Walter Scott, one day in Spring, was walking round Abbotsford with Lady Scott. Passing a field where there were a number of ewes and frolicking lambs, Sir Walter said (so the story goes):

'Ah, 'tis no wonder that poets, from the earliest ages, have made the lamb the emblem of peace and innocence.'

'Delightful animals, indeed,' rejoined Lady Scott, '—especially with mint sauce.'

DANIEL GEORGE

ARTISTS

*

Where others see but the dawn coming over the hill, I see the soul of God shouting for joy.

WILLIAM BLAKE

An artist may be a visionary, but his visions assume a livelier and more enduring shape than anything he sees around him.

Artists, like children, are excited by the irrational, the bizarre, and the outlandish.

AUGUSTUS JOHN

AUTHORS

After being turned down by numerous publishers, he decided to write for posterity.   GEORGE ADE

Authors in general are not good listeners.
WILLIAM HAZLETT

Only a mediocre writer is always at his best.
W. SOMERSET MAUGHAM

I do not like to think an author is trying to write a book. I like to imagine he is talking to me.
MADAME DU DEFFAND

The actual definition of reviewmanship is now, I think, stabilized. In its shortest form it is 'How to be one up on the author without actually tampering with the text'. In other words, how, as a critic, to show that it is really you yourself who should have written the book, if you had had the time, and since you hadn't, you are glad that someone else has, although obviously it might have been done better.
STEPHEN POTTER

No news is good news; no journalists is even better.
NICOLAS BENTLEY

A newspaper is a circulating library with high blood pressure.   ARTHUR BAER

The best way to become acquainted with a subject is to write a book about it.   BENJAMIN DISRAELI

A library should be a place into which you can be flung at any time and you will find your own pasturage.
STANLEY BALDWIN

I think it must be obvious why people always find authors disappointing. They want to meet an opus and they meet a man.

GEORGE MIKES

Manuscript : Something submitted in haste and returned at leisure.

OLIVER HERFORD

It took me fifteen years to discover that I had no talent for writing, but I couldn't give it up because by that time I was too famous.

ROBERT BENCHLEY

Journalists say a thing that they know isn't true, in the hope that if they keep on saying it long enough it *will* be true.

ARNOLD BENNETT

I couldn't write the things they publish now, with no beginning and no end, and a little incest in the middle.

IRVIN S. COBB

'Why is it that, in novels and newspapers blushes always "creep" over a girl's face?' 'Because if they ran, they'd kick up such a dust!'

AUTHORSHIP

Soon after Dominic Behan had his first play produced (and when his more famous brother Brendan had written several plays) Behan *pére* was asked if he were contemplating one.

He replied: 'Sure, what would I be producing plays for when I produce playwrights?'

BATHOS

*

Tideswell! thou art my natal spot
    And hence I love thee well;
May prosperous days now be the lot
    Of all that in thee dwell.

BEEBE EYRE

O Moon! When I look on thy beautiful face,
Careering along through the boundaries of space,
The thought has quite frequently come to my mind,
If ever I'll gaze on thy glorious behind.
    (*Lines written by Edmund Gose's housemaid,*
                before the age of luniks)

Over the wire the electric message came:
'He is not better, he much the same'.
    ALFRED AUSTIN, Poet Laureate (at the time
    when King Edward VII was seriously ill on
    the Riviera.)

BLESSINGS

*

If you don't get everything you want, think of the things you don't get that you don't want.

OSCAR WILDE

A blessing ought in truth to be the *more* satisfactory, the bounty at least of the donor is rendered more conspicuous, by its very diffusion, its commonness, its cheapness; by its falling to the lot, and forming the happiness, of the great bulk and body of our species, as well as of ourselves.

WILLIAM PALEY

Enjoy what you've got at the moment, and you'll find almost every moment brings something enjoyable.

ANON

'Now, children,' said the Sunday School teacher just before Christmas, briskly, 'tell me something you have to be thankful for.'

'I'm thankful,' said one small boy, 'that I'm *not* a turkey.'

BOOKS
*

Asked by her professor which book she would choose if she could have only one, a young woman student thought for a moment and then said: 'A cheque book'.

When asked a similar question Lord Birkett replied: 'The Oxford English Dictionary'.

*   *   *

In the main there are two sorts of books; those that no one reads and those that no one ought to read.

H. L. MENCKEN

I can read anything which I call a *book*.

CHARLES LAMB

I never read a book before reviewing it. It prejudices a man so.

SYDNEY SMITH

A man who attempts to read all the new productions must do as the flea does—skip.

SAMUEL ROGERS

'Pray, sir,' said Mr. Hume, 'in what branch of philosophy did you employ your researches? What books did you read?'

'Books?' said Mr. White. 'Nay, sir, I read no books, but I used to sit whole forenoons a'yawning and poking the fire.'

SIR DAVID DALRYMPLE

I've given up reading books; I find it takes my mind off myself.

OSCAR WILDE

I have met people who have borrowed my books from the library; I have met others, more enterprising, who have stolen them from the library; but I have never met anyone who has *bought* any of my books.

RUSSELL BRADDON (in 'Any Questions?')

Unprovided with original learning, unfound in the habits of thinking, unskilled in the arts of composition, I resolved —to write a book.

EDWARD GIBBON

To give an accurate and exhaustive account of that period would need a pen far less brilliant than mine.

SIR MAX BEERBOHM

None writes so ill that he gives not something exemplary to follow, to flie.

JOHN DONNE

Writing for problematic fame soon palls.

ARTHUR WAUGH

There is no book so bad but there is something good in it.

CERVANTES

I hate books; they only teach us to talk about things we know nothing about.

ROUSSEAU

I would never read a book if it were possible for me to talk half-an-hour with the man who wrote it.

WOODROW WILSON

In books cherubim expand their wings, that the soul of the student may ascend and look around from pole to pole, from the rising and the setting sun, from the north and from the sea.

RICHARD DE BURY (*Philobiblion*)

This books can do—nor this alone: they give new views to life, and teach us how to live; they soothe the grieved, the stubborn they chastise; fools they admonish, and confirm the wise.

GEORGE CRABBE

Reading is thinking with someone else's head instead of one's own.

SCHOPENHAUER

Of all odd crazes, the craze to be forever reading new books is one of the oddest.

AUGUSTINE BIRRELL

'What is the use of a book,' thought Alice, 'without pictures or conversations?'

LEWIS CARROLL

BOREDOM

*

When I get by myself, I undress myself and seem to have had people in my pockets, in my plaits, and on my shoulder. . . . I literally seem to have murdered a man whose name was Ennui, for his ghost is ever before me.

HORACE WALPOLE

We often forgive those who bore us, but we cannot forgive those whom we bore.

LA ROCHEFOUCAULD

A bore is a man who, when you ask him how he is, tells you.

ANON

Boredom is as great an evil as the exhaustion of the muscles.

DR. J. BRONOWSKI

Alexandre Dumas, *père*, was asked after a dinner party; 'Well, how did it go?'
'Not too well,' he replied. 'If I hadn't been there myself, I should have been bored to death.'

*   *   *

It is a tolerable depiction of a bore that he is one who talks about himself when you want to talk about yourself.

R. H. BENSON

There is nothing so insupportable to man as complete repose, without passion, occupation, amusement, care.

PASCAL

Boredom is dangerously infectious; and has a way of spreading across the footlights.

G. K. CHESTERTON

How soft, how snug, how warm, how comfortable—and how bored you are!

ANTON TCHEKHOV

An enthusiastic lover of insects had been talking to Mrs. Patrick Campbell about ants and their doings—and had bored her stiff in the process.

'You know,' he continued, 'ants have their own army and their own police force.'

Mrs. Campbell raised a languid eyebrow.

'No navy, I suppose?' she said..

*   *   *

O wad some power the giftie gie us to see some people before they see us.

ETHEL WATTS MUMFORD

CHILDREN

*

Tell your nice mummies and daddies to buy this book for you, and hit them until they do.

SPIKE MILLIGAN

I like some particular boys; but the genus boy seems ta me one of nature's mistakes.

LESLIE STEPHENS

I think I can say I had as unhappy a childhood as the next braggart.

PETER DE VRIES

It costs as much to amuse your child today as it once did to educate you.

Anon.

Little Girl: 'If I'm noisy they spank me—and if I'm quiet they take my temperature.

*   *   *

Infants' Department singing morning hymn:
     'We can sing, full though we be.'
     (Weak and sinful though we be.)

*   *   *

Mother (briefing her son before a party)
'Now be sure to thank Mrs. Robinson for having you, and tell her that you are sorry that you were so naughty!'

*   *   *

Little girl (given stewed rabbit again): 'Mummy, must I always have the part with the corsets on?'

Before I got married I had six theories about bringing up children; now I have six children and no theories.

JOHN WILMOT, Earl of Rochester

By the time the youngest children have learned to keep the house tidy, the oldest grandchildren are on hand to tear it to pieces again.

CHRISTOPHER MORLEY

A little girl was given a ring as a present. She put it on and went to see some friends, but none of them noticed it.
After a time she said: 'Oh, dear, I'm so warm in my new ring.'

*   *   *

I believe that the best luck is to be happily married, and the next best luck is to have good friends.

JAMES HILTON

Question: What were the principal cultural contributions of the Phoenicians?
Answer: Blinds.

*   *   *

If parents would only realize how they bore their children.

GEORGE BERNARD SHAW

Train your child in the way in which you know you should have gone yourself.

C. H. SPURGEON

Must one, after all, have a special attitude to childbirth? Do we need some defensive covering to pull over this run-of-the-mill process? I can't myself see that we do, for like all functions birth is only interesting by virtue of what it achieves. What matters, after all, is the baby who emerges hopping mad from the indignity of his journey, but responds to kindness with pathetic eagerness. Compared to him, birth is just a dull chore that nobody wants to hear about, and the sooner we stop regarding it as 'the supreme agony' (E. M. Forster), 'a quasi-mystical experience' (Dick-Reed), 'a beautiful event' (women's magazines), 'a great mystery' (my Vicar), or 'rather fun' (graduate wives), the better. It's a clever little bit of mechanics, that's all.

MONICA FURLONG

Anything which parents have not learned from experience they can now learn from their children.

Anon.

Parents were invented to make children happy by giving them something to ignore.

OGDEN NASH

A Sunday School is a prison in which children do penance for the evil conscience of their parents.

H. L. MENCKEN

Children begin by loving their parents; as they grow older they judge them; sometimes they forgive them.

OSCAR WILDE

The parent who could see his boy as he really is would shake his head and say : 'Willie is no good, I'll sell him.'

STEPHEN LEACOCK

Nothing offends children so much as to play down to them. GEORGE BERNARD SHAW

I was telling my nine-year-old granddaughter the story of the princess and the frog. 'When the little frog rescued her golden ball from the well, the princess was so grateful that she let him spend the night in her room,' I said. 'And the next morning when she woke up he had turned into a handsome prince and they were married and lived happily ever after.'

My granddaughter looked at me dubiously.

'Don't you believe the story?' I asked.

'No,' she replied, 'I don't. And I'll bet her mother didn't either.'

The Reader's Digest

A small girl was asked: 'Would you rather be good or beautiful?'

She answered: 'I think I'd rather be beautiful—and then repent.'

The world-wide fraternity of children is the greatest of savage tribes, and the only one which shows no sign of dying out.

DOUGLAS NEWTON

A mother had threatened her small son that Wee Willie Winkie would come for him if he did not go to sleep.

'No, he won't,' the child retorted, 'because I'm in bed, and God is in bed with me!'

CIVILIZATION

*

The origin of civilization is man's determination to do nothing for himself which he can get done for him.

H. C. BAILEY

Culture is the union of two things—fastidious taste and liberal sympathy.   W. H. MALLOCK

Increased means and increased leisure are the two civilizers of man.   BENJAMIN DISRAELI

To be cultivated, one must read slowly and with a lingering appreciation the comparatively few books which have been written by men who lived, thought, and felt with style.   ALDOUS HUXLEY

It needs civilization, it needs second thoughts, to realize that Napoleon and Caesar and Alexander are not really the highest types of humanity, that war-making is not a glory, but a crime.   GILBERT MURRAY

The ancient Greeks could not drive a motor-car at 300 miles an hour, or fly from Athens to England in a day. Their existence was not seriously impoverished by the inability. They could not broadcast the Aeschylean Trilogy; but they could write it. They possessed most, if not all, of the things which make human existence splendid and memorable.

SIR R. W. LIVINGSTONE

It is not too soon for us in our new world of mechanical civilization to take up once more the old search for wisdom.

GRAHAM WALLAS

Civilization is a slow process of adopting the ideas of minorities.   *Anon.*

CONVERSATION

*

He played with an idea and grew wilful, tossed it into the air and transformed it, let it escape and recaptured it, made it irridescent with fancy and winged it with paradox.

OSCAR WILDE

If every man were straightforward in his opinions there would be no conversation.

BENJAMIN DISRAELI

Contradiction and flattery both make poor conversation. ,

GOETHE

After all, the only proper intoxication is conversation.

OSCAR WILDE

Women have simple tastes. They can get pleasure out of the conversation of children in arms and men in love.

H. L. MENCKEN

Conversation between Adam and Eve must have been difficult at times because they had nobody to talk about.

AGNES REPPLIER

He has occasional flashes of silence that make his conversation perfectly delightful.

SYDNEY SMITH (of Macaulay)

The misfortune of Goldsmith in conversation is this: he goes on without knowing how he is to get off.

DR. JOHNSON

Very talkative lady (to Dr. Johnson): 'Why, Doctor, I believe you prefer the company of men to that of ladies.'

Dr. Johnson: 'Madam, I am very fond of the company of ladies; I like their beauty, I like their delicacy, I like their vivacity and I like their *silence*.'

* * *

After the age of forty conversation replaces love as a secondary cause of jealousy.

LORD VANSITTART

The secret of being tiresome is to tell everything.

VOLTAIRE

Don't knock the weather; nine-tenths of the people couldn't start a conversation if it didn't change once in a while.

FRANK M. HUBBARD

Your ignorance cramps my conversation.

ANTHONY HOPE

I never desire to converse with a man who has written more than he has read.

DR. JOHNSON

If you are ever at a loss to support a flagging conversation, introduce the subject of eating.

LEIGH HUNT

Drawing on my fine command of language, I said nothing.

ROBERT BENCHLEY

If one could only teach English how to talk and the French how to listen, society would be quite civilized.

OSCAR WILDE

No man would listen to you talk if he didn't know it was his turn next.

EDGAR W. HOWE

I am not fond of uttering platitudes in stained-glass attitudes.

W. S. GILBERT

'Really, when other people will talk, conversation becomes impossible!'

Men supposed to be educated may soon be unable to find any subject for conversation in which they can share except perhaps golf and bridge.

The Times

She was not a woman of many words; for unlike people in general she proportioned them to her ideas.

JANE AUSTEN

DEFINITIONS

*

He is every other inch a gentleman.

REBECCA WEST

A *financier* is a pawnbroker with imagination.

SIR ARTHUR PINERO

Free verse; the triumph of mind over metre.

Life

Bank: An institution which will lend you money if you can prove that you do not need it.   *Anon.*

Television: Chewing gum for the eyes.

FRANK LLOYD WRIGHT

Peace: A period of cheating between two periods of fighting.   AMBROSE BIERCE

Budget: A mathematical confirmation of your suspicions.   JOHN A. LINCOLN

Civilization is a movement and not a condition; a voyage and not a harbour.   ARNOLD TOYNBEE

A prig is a fellow who is always making you a present of his opinions.   GEORGE ELIOT

A Gentleman's Agreement is an arrangement which is not an agreement, between two persons, neither of whom is a gentleman, with each expecting the other to be strictly bound while he himself has no intention of being bound at all.   MR. JUSTICE VAISEY

Egoist: One who thinks that if he had not been born people would wonder why.

*   *   *

Cricket: Something the English—not being a naturally religious people—have had to invent to give them some idea of the eternal.   LORD MANCROFT

Fame: The advantage of being known to those who do not know us.   NICHOLAS CHAMFORT

Tact consists in knowing how far we may go too for.
                                        JEAN COCTEAU

Tact: Putting out your psychic and intellectual antennae.

The first ROTARIAN was the first man to call John the Baptist Jack.   H. L. MENCKEN

Love is the delusion that one woman differs from another.
                                        ibid

Gentleman: One who never strikes a woman without provocation.   *ibid*

Repartee: Any reply that is so clever that it makes the listener wish he had said it himself.
                                        ELBERT HUBBARD

Bore: A man who is never unintentionally rude.
                                        OSCAR WILDE

Scandal is gossip made tedious by morality.
                                        OSCAR WILDE

'*O & M*' expert: A man who first learns your job, and

then, in return for a large fee, shows you how it can be dispensed with.

*   *   *

Aristocracy : Government by the best men. (In this sense the word is obsolete; so is that kind of government.)

AMBROSE BIERCE

Auctioneer : The man who proclaims with a hammer that he has picked a pocket with his tongue.

Architect : One who drafts a plan of your house and plans a draft of your money.

ibid

Backbite : To speak of a man as you find him when he can't find you.

ibid

Highbrow : The kind of person who looks at a sausage and thinks of Picasso.

SIR ALAN HERBERT

Cynic : A man who tells you the truth about your own motives.

RUSSELL GREEN

Policeman : A never-present help in time of trouble.

*   *   *

Psychiatrist : A man who will listen to you so long as you don't make sense.

*   *   *

Diplomacy : Diplomacy is the art of letting someone have your way.

DANIELE VARÉ

An egotist is a man who expects a woman to marry him for himself alone.   *Anon.*

Lisp: To call a spade a thpade.

OLIVER HERFORD

Genius: The capacity of seeing something from an angle that no one saw it from before; or a kind of luminous sanity.

Modesty: The gentle art of enhancing your charm by pretending not to be aware of it.   *ibid*

Jade: A semi-precious stone or a semi-precious woman.
                                                      ibid

Song: The licenced medium for bawling in public things too silly or sacred to be uttered in ordinary speech.
                                                      ibid

Zoo: A place devised for animals to study the habits of human beings.   *ibid*

Atheist: A man who has no invisible means of support.
JOHN BUCHAN

Admiration: Our polite recognition of another man's resemblance to ourselves.

AMBROSE BIERCE

Bore: (1) A person who talks when you wish him to listen.

                                                      ibid
            (2) One who makes others take the world seriously.

LORD VANSITTART

Hen: Only an egg's way of making another egg.
S. BUTLER

DOCTORS

*

The art of medicine consists in amusing the patient while
nature cures the disease.

VOLTAIRE

Doctors pour drugs of which they know little, to cure
diseases of which they know less, into human beings of
whom they know nothing. *ibid*

A woman went to see her doctor about a stomach ail-
ment. ''At's bin natterin' me summat chronic. Eh! An' I
wor dowly! I'd t'ditherum-dotherums all a' t' dea . . .'

When I was young, there were children's doctors but
no paediatricians, ear-nose-and-throat surgeons but no
orthinolaryngologists, skin doctors but no dermatologists,
mad doctors but no psychiatrists.

SIR ERNEST GOWERS

Doctors will have more lives to answer for in the next
world than even we generals.

NAPOLEON BUONAPARTE

There are only two sorts of doctors: those who practise
with their brains, and those who practise with their
tongues. SIR WILLIAM OSLER

They murmured as they took their fees,
'There is no cure for this disease.'

HILAIRE BELLOC

Doctors, like lawyers can be got to take opposing views.
But while a judge is able to pronounce which lawyer is

wrong, they only find out which doctor is wrong when the undertaker calls.

JAMES WALKER

My father often boasted that when he left medical school he knew a little anatomy, less physiology and one drug, ipecac.

S. W. VANDEGRIFT

> You say, without reward or fee
> Your remedy cured me of a dangerous ill:
> I say, he never did prescribe for me—
> The proof is plain, you see I'm living still.
>
> *Anon.*

'I've got five children, doctor, and I don't know what to do with them. What shall I do?'
'I would advise you to take three aspirins.'
'*When*, doctor—before or after?'
'Instead.'

*   *   *

Doctor (to clumsy anaesthetist): 'Mr. Anaesthetist, if the patient can keep awake, surely you can!'

A doctor met a young man at a cocktail party. 'I want to thank you, doctor,' said the latter, 'for the benefit I have gained from your treatment.'
The other looked at him blankly. 'But—er—' he said. 'I don't think you've ever been a patient of mine.'
'No, but my uncle was. I'm his heir.'

DONS

*

The famous Oxford philosopher, Dr F. H. Bradley, had a tyre puncture when he was cycling to a lecture. He leaned his bicycle against the front wall of St John's College, fitted the pump and proceeded to blow.

'Excuse me, sir,' said a passer-by, 'but you are blowing up your front tyre and it's the back tyre which has the puncture.'

'Dear me,' said Bradley, 'er—don't they communicate?'

*   *   *

Oscar Browning, whose *snobismes* amused his contemporaries at Cambridge, is reputed to have said after a visit by the Emperor Franz Joseph to the University: 'He was one of the nicest Emperors I have ever met!'

DREAMS

*

Existence would be intolerable if we were never to dream.

ANATOLE FRANCE

A child, awakened out of a deep sleep, expressed all the crying babies and all the weeping idealists in the world. 'Oh, dear,' he said, 'I have lost my place in my dream.'

LINCOLN STEFFENS

Don't tell me what you dreamed last night for I've been reading Freud.

FRANKLIN PIERCE ADAMS

Yesterday morning I awoke from a dream of peace compounded of equal parts of allonal and Vat 90 to find that Autumn was indeed here.

S. J. PERELMAN

'George Moore is ill in bed from a nightmare in which he thought the Germans had invaded England and were storming his bedroom—he jumped out of bed with the intention of resisting to the last, and slipped right along the floor to the other end of the room, cutting himself all to bits. He wants Maud (Cunard) to get him the vc on the ground that anybody can be brave when they're awake, but to be brave in one's sleep is the *real thing*.'

SIR EDWARD MARSH (in a letter)
(From Sir Edward Marsh by Christopher Hassall)

DRESS AND FASHION

*

Fashion : A despot whom the wise ridicule—and obey.
                                        AMBROSE BIERCE

Dylan Thomas used to say that his sartorial appearance
was that of an unmade bed.

*   *   *

No woman is ever too tired to put on a new dress.

*   *   *

You couldn't tell if she were dressed for an opera or an
operation.   IRVIN S. COBB

Brevity is the soul of lingerie.
                                        DOROTHY PARKER

I hold that gentlemen to be best dressed whose dress no
one observes.   ANTHONY TROLLOPE

I like to walk down Bond Street thinking of all the things
I don't want.
                                        LOGAN PEARSALL SMITH

. . . a frock that is made at home and repented at
leisure.   SAKI

The trouble about most Englishwomen is that they will
dress as if they had been a mouse in a previous incarnation,
or hope to be one in the next.
                                        DAME EDITH SITWELL

ECCENTRICS

*

John Fitzgerald's* fortune allowed him to indulge such absurdities as that of having a clock in every room at Boulge Hall, yet when he wanted to know the time to call for a valet to tell him. He would march into 'The Bull' at Woodbridge and order a carriage to take him back to Boulge, and then walk the whole way home with the carriage following.

JAMES TURNER

Lord Rokeby lived chiefly on beef-tea and was an enthusiastic water-drinker. He abhorred fires, and had a bath so constructed as to be warmed by the rays of the sun, and passed much of his time in it.

*   *   *

He pasted picture post-cards around goldfish bowls to make the goldfish think they were going places.

FRED ALLEN

A progressive society needs the eccentric.

Anon.

Canon Spooner, seeing his wife off from Oxford, is said to have kissed the porter and given his wife twopence.

* Brother of Edward Fitzgerald.

EDUCATION

*

Soap and education are not as sudden as a massacre but they are more deadly in the long run.

MARK TWAIN

What we want to see is the child in pursuit of knowledge, and not knowledge in pursuit of the child, cane in hand.

GEORGE BERNARD SHAW

A school party had been into the village on a coach trip, and the talk in the local turned on to modern life and education.

'Nay,' said one old fellow in the corner, as he leaned over to a man who could have been forty years younger, 'we make nowt of eddication up here, lad. We just uses our brains instead.'

The Dalesman

My education was so sound that I know hardly anything.

RONALD MACKENZIE

Education is an admirable thing, but it is well to remember from time to time that nothing that is worth knowing can be taught.

OSCAR WILDE

I would put a child in a library (where no unfit books are) and let him read at his choice.

DR. JOHNSON

The advantage of a classical education is that it enables you to despise the wealth which it prevents you from achieving.

RUSSELL GREEN

The general principles of any study you may learn by books at home; but the detail, the colour, the air, the life which makes it live in us—you must catch all those from those in whom it lives already.

CARDINAL NEWMAN

Nothing can be taught : all the teacher can do is to show that there are paths. *Anon.*

Training is everything. The peach was once a bitter almond. Cauliflower is nothing but cabbage with a college education.

MARK TWAIN

Nothing is easier in America than to attend College and nothing harder than to get educated.

DOUGLAS WOODRUFF

You have to go to a very good school indeed in order to avoid being taught any science at all.

LORD JAMES, High Master of Manchester
Grammar School

A Bishop went to address the boys at his old school. He took as his subject Moral Courage.

'Suppose,' he said, 'that twelve boys were sleeping in one dormitory, and before they went to sleep eleven of those boys jumped straight into bed, but one of them knelt down and said his prayers—that boy would afford a splendid example of Moral Courage.'

Some months afterwards the Bishop paid another visit to the school. Anxious to see if his address had made any lasting impression, he asked one boy :

'Do you remember the talk I gave you when I was last here?'

'Yes, my Lord,' the boy replied. 'It was about Moral Courage.'

'Well, can you give me an example of Moral Courage?'

'Oh, yes, my Lord. Suppose that twelve Bishops were at a Conference where they had to sleep in one dormitory, and before they went to sleep eleven of those Bishops knelt down and said their prayers, but one of them jumped straight into bed—that Bishop would be a splendid example of Moral Courage!'

The test of a truly educated man is what he is, and what he thinks, and what his mind absorbs, or dreams, or creates, when he is alone.

DONALD DAVID

I assure you that the number of things which I and my poor dear sister were taught *not* to understand was quite extraordinary.   OSCAR WILDE

Headmaster's comment at the end of schoolboy's report: 'Dull but steady—would make a good parent.'

*   *   *

'Billy,' said an exasperated Dales schoolteacher, during a lesson in composition. 'You've put "Putten" when you know very well you should have putten "Put".'

The Dalesman

Schoolmaster: 'It is possible that the whole of life began with some form of jelly.'

Pupil: 'What flavour?'

*   *   *

Mother (to her daughter back from her first day at school): 'Well, dear, what did they teach you?'

Daughter: Not much, Mum—I've got to go again to-morrow.'

*   *   *

I mean it seems to me a gentleman who has a friendly interest in educating a girl like Gus Eisman, would want her to have the biggest square cut diamond in New York.

ANITA LOOS

Limerick

> A tutor who tooted the flute
> Tried to tutor two tooters to toot,
>   Said the two to the tutor
>   'Is it harder to toot or
> To tutor two tooters to toot?'

Anon.

'Whom are you?' said he, for he had been to night school.

GEORGE ADE

In examinations the foolish ask questions that the wise cannot answer.

OSCAR WILDE

The Universities are a sort of lunatic asylum for keeping young men out of mischief.

BISHOP CREIGHTON

EGOTISM

*

Waterloo in retrospect:

He* repeated so often its being 'so nice a thing—so nearly run a thing' that I asked him if the French had fought better than he had ever seen them do before.

'No,' he said, 'they have always fought the same since I first saw them at Vimeiro.' Then he said: 'By God! I don't think it would have done if I had not been there.'

From the Creevey Papers

What men, in their egoism, constantly mistake for a deficiency of intelligence in woman is merely an incapacity for mastering that mass of small intellectual tricks, that complex of pretty knowledge, that collection of cerebral rubber stamps, which constitute the chief mental equipment of the average male.

H. L. MENCKEN

I never repeat anyone except myself.

RUSSELL GREEN

* The Duke of Wellington.

THE ENGLISH

*

An Englishman thinks he is moral when he is only uncomfortable.

GEORGE BERNARD SHAW

An Englishman does everything on principle: he fights you on patriotic principles; he robs you on business principles; he enslaves you on imperial principles.

ibid

Napoleon described the English as a nation of shopkeepers. He would have come nearer the truth if he had described them as a nation of goalkeepers.

ROBERT LYND

A fine, handsome specimen of British manhood, standing every bit of six foot two in his shoes, and fearing nothing but closing time.

ARTHUR M. BINSTEAD

'It is true that it sounds a little narcissistic, but I must tell you of a funny thing I learnt about the English when I was trying to learn your language. In English "I" am the only person allowed a capital no matter where I happen to be in the sentence: "You" are not worthy of capitals, nor "he" nor "she" nor "it" nor "they", not even "we".'

PETER MAYNE

1942: A critical year for Britain, with British Generals slaving away at their autobiographies.

From THE GOON SHOW

EPITAPHS

*

Epitaph : A belated advertisement for a line of goods that has been permanently discontinued.

IRVIN S. COBB

Reading the epitaphs, our only salvation lies in resurrecting the dead and burying the living..

PAUL ELDRIDGE

The rarest quality in an epitaph is truth.

A. D. THOREAU

Ci -git ma femme : oh! qu'elle est bien
Pour son repos et pour le mien.

JACQUES DU LORENS

ON ALDERMAN W——
THE HISTORY OF HIS LIFE
That he was born it cannot be denied,
He ate, drank, slept, talk'd politics, and died.

JOHN CUNNINGHAM

EXAMINATIONS

*

Member of the Board of Examiners at medical examination:

'Can you identify those three bones, Mr. Smith?'

Despairing Candidate: 'Gentlemen, for anything I know, they might be Faith, Hope and Charity!'

*　　*　　*

Father to schoolboy (who, in a mixed class, has come out below a schoolgirl in the terminal exams):

'Surely you haven't been beaten by a mere girl?'

Schoolboy: 'But, you know, pater, girls *aren't* so mere now as they were in *your* young days!'

*　　*　　*

Question: 'What is the use of the skin?'

Answer: 'The use of the skin is to hold the bones together, and to give you a better complexion.'

*　　*　　*

Question: 'Why is the neck of a giraffe so long?'

Answer: 'Because his head is so far away from his body.'

*　　*　　*

Question: 'What do you consider the greatest achievement of the ancient Romans?'

Answer: 'Speaking Latin.'

*　　*　　*

'Who are the three greatest sailors in British history?' asked an Admiral who was conducting an examination for the Navy.

Replied the candidate: 'I didn't catch your name when I entered the room, sir, but the other two are Nelson and Drake.'

THE FAIR SEX

*

A really 'dumb' woman is surely one who is not even thinking the things she is *not* saying.

MICHAEL BARCLAY

No man is a match for a woman except with a poker and a pair of hobnailed boots. .

GEORGE BERNARD SHAW

Women are not much but they are the best other sex we have.

DON HEROLD

The only way any woman may remain forever young is to grow old gracefully.

W. BÉRAN-WOLFE

The female woman is one of the greatest institooshuns of which this land can boste.

ARTEMUS WARD

There is only one thing worse than one dame, and that is two dames.

PETER CHEYNEY

There are only two kinds of women—the plain and the coloured.   OSCAR WILDE

She was one of those women who have gender but no sex.

J. F. SCOGGIN

Woman is a miracle of divine contradictions.

MICHELET

To live with women may impair a man's usefulness. To live without them, on the other hand, is bound to result in his being of no use at all.

MARMADUKE DIXEY

To a woman of spirit the most intolerable of all grievances is a restraint on the liberty of the tongue.

Anon.

'I think I could be a good woman if I had £5,000 a year.'
W. M. THACKERAY
(Becky Sharp in *Vanity Fair*)

A woman's mind is cleaner than a man's; she changes it more often.

OLIVER HERFORD

Here's to women! Would that we could fall into her arms without falling into her hands.

AMBROSE BIERCE

A woman can keep one secret—the secret of her age.

VOLTAIRE

A woman is fascinated not by art, but by the noise made by those who are in the art field.

TCHEKHOV

That woman's art-jargon tires me. . . . she's so fond of talking of certain pictures as 'growing on one', as though they were a sort of fungus.   SAKI'

The ladies looked one another over with microscopic carelessness.

ARTHUR BAER

A man reserves his greatest and deepest love not for the woman in whose company he finds himself electrified and enkindled, but for that one in whose company he may feel tenderly drowsy.

GEORGE JEAN NATHAN

The most relentless thing in life is a true love.

Anon.

'She turned you down? Never mind, old boy, a woman's "No" means nothing.'
. . . 'But she didn't say "No". She said "No fear!" '

* * *

One woman to another at party: 'I've heard so much about you! Now I'd like to hear your side of the story.'

* * *

She told him it was terrible to hear such things as he told her and to please go ahead.

GEORGE ADE

Women now insist on having all the prerogatives of the oak and all the perquisites of the clinging vine.

IRVIN S. COBB

I never expected to see the days when girls get sunburned in the places they now do.

WILL ROGERS

'Haven't spoken to my wife for weeks.'
'Why? Had a row?'
'No. I'm afraid to interrupt her.'

* * *

If you want to know what a woman really means look at her—do not listen to her.   OSCAR WILDE

The tyranny of woman is the worse form of tyranny the world has ever known—the tyranny of the weak over the strong.

OSCAR WILDE

Men marry because they are bored; women because they are curious: both are disappointed.

OSCAR WILDE

As I say when I talk to Women's Guilds: 'Ladies, I'm single. I go to bed to *sleep*.' Wait for the laugh. Then: 'Well, I know of men who go to bed to *read*.'

FRED BASON

There is something enchanting in English women. Beneath their cool dignity they have a streak of craziness which is wonderful.

ROGER VADIM

Typist (to friend): 'But don't ever tell him that you're not that kind of girl—he may believe you!'

*   *   *

She had the mouth that smiles in repose.

GEORGE MEREDITH

FILMS

*

I've had several years in Hollywood and I still think the movie heroes are in the audience.

WILSON MIZNER

She's going to make some man a good wife someday, provided he comes down off the movie screen and asks her.

THORNTON WILDER

What I am waiting for is a film about beautiful identical quintuplets who all love the same man.

RICHARD WINNINGTON

It is the business of Hollywood to shape the truth into box office contours.

*   *   *

Small boy: 'Oh, the film wasn't much good, Mum, but it was worth the money to see Aunt Ethel's face!'

*   *   *

'It made me laugh a great deal and cry a little—which is my simple criterion for a good film.'

*   *   *

A film actress was applying for a passport.
'Unmarried?' asked the clerk.
'Occasionally,' she replied.

*   *   *

American motion-pictures are written by the half-educated for the half-witted.

ST JOHN ERVINE

In the early days of the film industry a Yorkshire cinema owner, whose knowledge of showmanship was greater than his knowledge of English, received a telephone call from the manager of his biggest and most prosperous picture palace.

'Patrons are complaining that there are fleas in this theatre,' ran the call.

The Great One got into his Rolls-Royce and drove straight to the cinema. He strode on to the middle of the stage.

'Stop t'pitchers! Stop t'orchestra!' he roared. 'Aw'm told,' he added, jutting out his jaw at the audience, 'that you say there's fleas in this 'ere theayter. If there's fleas in this 'ere theayter yer browt 'em yersens. Start t'pitchers! Start t'orchestra!'

And he strolled back to his Rolls-Royce.

The Dalesman

When she entered a cinema with her dog in her arms an attendant stepped forward. 'Excuse me, madam,' he said, 'but you can't take your dog inside.'

'How absurd!' protested the woman. 'What harm could the pictures do to a tiny dog like this?'

FOOD AND DRINK

*

After a good dinner, one can forgive anybody, even one's own relatives.

OSCAR WILDE

God never sendeth mouth but he sendeth meat.
JOHN HEYWOOD

There are nine ways of poaching eggs, and each of them is worse than the other.

ROBERT LYND

The following epitaph was written upon Dr. Thomas Sergeant, a Fellow of All Souls in the 17th century:
'Here lyes Dr. Sergeant within the cloysters,
 Whom if the last trump don't waken, then crye oysters.'
The doctor would never answer or come to anyone hardly that come to his door; . . . 'but if a crye of oysters was raised he would immediately come out, being a great admirer of them, as indeed he was of other good eatables as well as drinkables.'

*   *   *

As a prolonged drinking party in Scotland, one of the guests remarked: 'What gaes the laird of Garskadden sae gast?'*
'Oh,' says his neighbour, the laird of Kilmardinny, 'deil meane him! Garskadden's been wi' his Maker these two hours; I saw him step awa, but I didna like to disturb guide company!'

*   *   *

* Ghastly.

A beadle was being examined as an unwilling witness in a case where a Scottish minister was charged with drunkenness.

He was asked: 'Did you ever see the minister the worse of drink?'

'I cannot say I've seen him the worse o' drink, but nae doubt I've seen him the better o't,' he replied.

Two of the many processes in the cutlery trade are known as 'roughing down' and 'polishing' a blade or knife.

At the annual dinner of one cutlery firm, a workman placed a chicken leg, from which most of the meat had been cut, on his neighbour's plate, and said:

' 'Ere, lad, thee polish this one off while I rough tha' another one darn!'

* * *

We all know that dinners are occupational hazards for Lord Mayors.

THE DUKE OF EDINBURGH

* * *

When that rising author John Bacchus developed chronic alcoholism, he earnestly pursued a cure—homeopathic treatment.

RUSSELL GREEN

Tell me what you eat and I will tell you what you are.
BRILLAT-SAVARIN

Good Food Needs no Accompaniment.

Diner (to orchestra leader): 'Could you play something by request?'

Leader: 'Why, certainly, sir.'

Diner: 'Then go and play draughts until I've finished eating.'

* * *

On the Continent people have good food, in England people have good table manners.

GEORGE MIKES

English Picnic—Indoors.
'Everything as natural and simple as possible. Is not that your idea?'
'Not quite. My idea of the simple and natural will be to have the table spread in the dining room. The nature and the simplicity of gentlemen and ladies, with their servants and furniture, I think is best observed by meals within doors. When you are tired of eating strawberries in the garden, there shall be cold meat in the house.'

JANE AUSTEN

A man is in general better pleased when he has a good dinner on his table than when his wife talks Greek.

DR. JOHNSON

Absinthe makes the heart grow fonder.

ADDISON MIZNER

Abstainer: A weak person who yields to the temptation of denying himself a pleasure.

AMBROSE BIERCE

Drinking makes such fools of people, and people are such fools to begin with that it's compounding a felony.

ROBERT BENCHLEY

The great majority of the English move inside much too narrow an orbit of drink, and many live more between tea and beer.

DOUGLAS WOODRUFF

Drink because you are happy, but never because you are miserable.

G. K. CHESTERTON

I must get out of these wet clothes and into a dry martini.
ALEXANDER WOOLLCOTT

Lo! the poor toper whose untutor'd sense
Sees bliss in ale, and can with wine dispense;
Whose head proud fancy never taught to steer
Beyond the muddy ecstasies of beer.
GEORGE CRABBE

Only a genius can sparkle on water.
SIR SEYMOUR HICKS

I am sure that moderate drinking makes men talk better.
SIR JOSHUA REYNOLDS

Man in all periods has been willing to walk miles for a
drink, but not for a bath.
LAWRENCE WRIGHT

'A man who can really give a good dinner has learned a
great deal,' said Lord Dumbello, with unusual animation.
'An immense deal. It is quite an art in itself: and one
which I, at any rate, by no means despise. But we cannot
always be eating—can we?'
'No,' said Lord Dunbello, 'not always.' And he looked as
though he lamented that his powers should be so circum-
scribed.   ANTHONY TROLLOPE

For each composer he liked to dispense the appropriate
drink: for Mozart, champagne; for Schubert, claret; for
Wagner, beer; for Mahler, tea. Beethoven, he said, was too
great to be played except in solitude.
R. C. ROBERTSON-GLASGOW

A man told a friend, at great length, about his wife's
special chocolate cake. His detail was perfect, his descrip-
tion vivid. 'Then,' he concluded, 'she takes a strawberry
and puts it in the middle of the cake.'

'And is it good?' asks the friend.
The man shakes his head. 'No!' he says, sadly.

SIR BEVERLEY BAXTER

He who can make a perfect omelette can probably do nothing else.

HILAIRE BELLOC

'Such poor liquor do make a man's throat feel very melancholy—and is a disgrace to the name of stimmilant.'

THOMAS HARDY

'When my husband doesn't feel well, he drinks, and when he drinks, he doesn't feel well.'

Woman at Police Court

If you ask an Englishman to have a drink, what does he reply? He replies, 'I don't mind if I do.' What he really means is, 'I shall mind if I don't.'

*　　*　　*

'. . . a glass of whine.'

HERMIONE GINGOLD

It would be an awful thing if the ancient drinks were forgotten during the tyranny of the chocolate-makers, Quakers, or whoever they were dried a great nation. Gin is the enemy of good drink. I suppose no American can remember what good claret tasted like. To whom would he go to recover the lost taste?

OLIVER ST JOHN GOGARTY

An old Scottish lady offered a carpenter, who was working for her, a dram of whisky, and asked him whether he would have it then or wait till his work was done.

'Indeed, mem,' he said, 'there's been sic a power o' sudden death lately that I'll just tak it now.'

A junior minister having to assist at a church in a remote part of Aberdeenshire, the parochial minister (one of the old school) promised his young friend a good glass of whisky-toddy after all was over, adding slyly 'and gude *smuggled* whisky.'

His Southern guest felt it incumbent to say: 'Ah, minister, that's wrong, is it not? You know it is contrary to Act of Parliament.'

'Oh,' said the old Aberdonian, 'Acts of Parliament lose their breath before they get to Aberdeenshire.'

DEAN RAMSAY

No man ever pulled himself out of his troubles with a corkscrew.

HIS HONOUR J. TUDOR REES

I ne'er had any love yet that I could not satisfye with Gold or wash away with Burgundy.

SHADWELL

The Prima Donna, smiling herself out,
Recruits her flagging powers with bottled stout.

C. S. CALVERLEY

GAMES

*

Lord Braxfield, at whist, exclaimed to a lady with whom he was playing: 'What are you doing, ye damned auld ...?', and then recollecting himself: 'Your pardon's begged, Madam. I took ye for my ain wife.'

THOMAS BABINGTON MACAULAY

'I wonder why Scotsmen are so good at golf?'
'Well, you see, they realize that the fewer times they strike the ball, the longer it will last!'

*   *   *

Golfer (to caddie): 'Why the dickens didn't you keep your eye on where my ball went?'
Caddie: 'Well, sir, it don't usually go anywhere, so it took me unprepared, like.'

*   *   *

Lord Russell of Killowen, when Lord Chief Justice, was playing bridge at his club and had a young subaltern as his partner. The subaltern made some mistakes in his play and Lord Russell complained in no mild terms.
'Remember, Lord Russell,' his partner remarked, 'you're not in your blooming police court now!'

*   *   *

In the tennis world, there is a major difference between the professional and the amateur. The amateur, unlike the

professional, insists on being paid *before* he appears on the
court.   E. HORSFALL TURNER

The coldness of a losing gamester lessens the pleasure of
the winner. I'd no more play with a man that slighted his
ill fortune then I'd make love to a woman who under-
valued the loss of her reputation.

WILLIAM CONGREVE

When Yorkshire plays Lancashire *expertise* is as rife
as partisanship. They tell the story of a stranger who
applauded both sides in quick succession and was looked at
askance by his neighbours.

'Are thee Yorkshire?' asked one.
'No.'
'Are thee Lancashire?' asked the other.
'No.'
'Then mind own bloody business,' said both together.

It is almost impossible to remember how tragic a place
the world is when one is playing golf.

ROBERT LYSAT

Games lubricate the body and the mind.
BENJAMIN FRANKLIN

I am afraid I play no outdoor games at all, except
dominoes. I have sometimes played dominoes outside
French cafés.   OSCAR WILDE

Play is one of the main bases of civilization.
JOHAN HUIZINGE

Boat Race: All rowed fast, but none so fast as stroke.
OUIDA

'You asked what trumps were at least a dozen times,' a man complained to his wife on the way back from a bridge party.

'Yes, dear, I know,' she said, 'but I didn't really have to—I just wanted to show everybody that I was taking an interest in the game.'

HAPPINESS

*

It is not the possession of good things which brings happiness—it is the ability to enjoy what comes. Happiness is an aptitude.

BERNARD GRASSET

Perfect happiness is the absence of striving for happiness.

CHUANG-TSE

Happiness and beauty are by-products.

GEORGE BERNARD SHAW

Some of us might find happiness if we quit struggling so desperately for it.

WILLIAM FEATHER

All happiness depends on courage and work.

HONORE DE BALZAC

It's pretty hard to tell what brings happiness; poverty and wealth have both failed.

F. M. HUBBARD

When I was young I thought that money was the most important thing in life; now that I am old I know that it is.

OSCAR WILDE

. . . that sanguine expectation of happiness which is happiness itself.

JANE AUSTEN

Happiness consists of intense activity in congenial surroundings. SIR HAROLD NICOLSON

Happiness, I have discovered, is nearly always a rebound from hard work.

DAVID GRAYSON

A happy man may be a successful bishop, dog-catcher, movie actor or sausage-monger, but no happy man ever produced a first-rate piece of painting, sculpture, music or literature.　　　　　　　　　　　　　　J. G. NATHAN

The easy, open, fortunate man is the likeable man, the kindly man, the considerate man—in short, the man who may have time and inclination to think of someone beside himself. Be virtuous, and you'll be happy? Nonsense! Be happy, and you'll begin to be virtuous.

J. G. COZZENS

The greatest pleasure I know is to do a good action by stealth and have it found out by accident.

CHARLES LAMB

To love and to be loved the wise would give
All that for which alone the unwise live.

W. S. LANDOR

The search for happiness is one of the chief sources of unhappiness.

ERIC HOFFER

All the things I really like to do are either immoral, illegal or fattening.

ALEXANDER WOOLLCOTT

You cannot attain happiness by seeking it, or willing it. Happiness just happens.　　　　　　　　　　　　　　*Anon.*

I have learnt to seek my happiness in limiting my desires rather than in attempting to satisfy them.

JOHN STUART MILL

The secret of happiness is curiosity.

NORMAN DOUGLAS

The two most hopeful foundations for happiness are,
first, work (and plenty of it); secondly, affection.

F. L. LUCAS

The good end happily, the bad unhappily—that is what
fiction means.

OSCAR WILDE

The secret of happiness is to admire without desiring.
And that is not happiness.

DR. F. H. BRADLEY

He had a genius for happiness and for spreading happiness around him, and it was remarkable that neither the
greater nor the lesser pleasures of his life ever palled on
him, as on so many they do; to him his successes, his popularity, his possessions, never grew stale or flat or unprofit-
able—he turned naturally to the light like a flower..

SIR EDWARD MARSH (on Ivor Novello)

Some few there be, spoilt darlings of high Heaven,
To whom the magic grace of charm is given.

SIR EDWARD MARSH (translation of
La Fontaine)

There has probably very rarely ever been so happy a
position as that of a London private banker; and never
perhaps a happier.

WALTER BAGEHOT

HEALTH AND SICKNESS

*

On Gout: Cherubims that have no legs and do nothing but stick their chins in a cloud and sing, are never out of order.

HORACE WALPOLE

He had insomnia so bad that he couldn't sleep when he was working.

ARTHUR BAER

'I've just learned about his illness, let's hope it's nothing trivial.'

IRVIN S. COBB

Drink wine and have the gout; drink none and have the gout.   THOMAS COGAN

I do not know a single person, whose intellect I respect, who enjoys robust health.

SIR PETER CHALMERS-MITCHELL

'How is your wife getting on, John?'
'Well, sir, sometimes she's better and sometimes she's worse. But from the way she takes on when she's better, oi be thinking she's better when she's worse.'

*   *   *

I heard a Darwin story the other day that I liked: the butler was overheard saying to a visiting maid, 'Master thinks he's ill, but it's my opinion if he had something to occupy his mind with he'd be all right.'

JANE HARRISON

A doctor subjected one of his patients to a thorough examination, or at least 'went through the motions' of doing so. When he had finished, he said to the patient's garrulous wife:

'He's not really seriously ill. All he needs now is a bit of peace and quiet—I suggest he goes back to work.'

* * *

A patient told a psychiatrist that he could not remember anything for more than a few minutes at a time.

'How long has this been going on?' asked the psychiatrist.

'How long has *what* been going on?' replied the man.

* * *

A woman was trying to find the ward of a large hospital where a friend of hers was recuperating from an operation. After walking along a corridor for a few hundred yards she saw a man wearing a white coat and said: 'Excuse me, but are you a doctor?'

'No,' he said, 'I'm a student passing out for a doctor,' and walked on.

So she continued her walk and after a few minutes met another man wearing a white coat and said: 'Excuse me, are *you* a doctor?'

'No,' he replied. 'I'm a student passing out for a doctor,' and walked on.

After a few more hundred yards she met a third man wearing a white coat, and, determined to detain him and ask where the ward was, said: 'Excuse me, are you a student passing out for a doctor?'

'No,' he replied, 'I'm a painter passing out for a pint.'

* * *

Many people live their lives in an atmosphere of slight nausea, produced by constant overdoses, first of one thing and then of its antidote. GILBERT MURRAY

'I've finished with my psychiatrist,' said a young woman. 'I may be a case, but I can't get used to a man who keeps on telling me to lie down on the couch—and then sends *me* the bill.

* * *

What I call a good patient is one who, having found a good physician, sticks to him till he dies.

OLIVER WENDELL HOLMES

Ugliness is a point of view; an ulcer is wonderful to a pathologist.

AUSTIN O'MALLEY

Tee or Tea?
'Give me your candid advice, Doctor.'
'I will. I'd advise you to give up your golfing and spend more time at the office.'

* * *

Chemists are so overworked today that their life is just sheer druggery.

* * *

God heals, and the doctor takes the fee.

BENJAMIN FRANKLIN

Doctors know what you tell them.

DON HEROLD

For every disease that doctors cure with medicine they produce ten in healthy people by inoculating them with that virus which is a thousand times more powerful than any microbe: the idea that one is ill.

MARCEL PROUST

The doctor had called to see a railway signalman who had been off duty with rheumatism. After examining him the doctor remarked : 'It would be a good thing if you took a bath before you retire.'

'Nay,' said the railwayman. 'That's a long time to wait. Ah don't retire for another ten years.'

The Dalesman

A sick man went to the chemist with some prescriptions from his doctor. The chemist explained to him :

'You have three kinds of pills here : one to soothe your nerves, another to take away your headache, and the third to calm your stomach.'

The man was filled with wonder.

'Please tell me,' he said, 'how on earth can three little pills know just where to go?'

* * *

An elderly farmer in these parts has for some time past been receiving special treatment for his rheumatism. The treatment has been effective, and a little while ago the doctor told him he could regard himself as better.

Naturally there have been many callers to congratulate him on his cure. One looked in the other morning. 'Now, Mr Smith, I reckon tha's fair set up wi' thissen now tha's getten rid o' t'rheumatics.'

'Nay, I don't know so much,' replied the old chap. 'Tha sees I can't tell now when it's going to rain.'

The Dalesman

HEAVEN AND HELL

*

Heaven is the place where the donkey finally catches up with his carrot: Hell is the eternity while he waits for it.

RUSSELL GREEN

What is hell? Hell is oneself,
Hell is alone, the other figures in it
Merely projections. There is nothing to escape from
And nothing to escape to. One is always alone.

T. S. ELIOT

Hell is other people.

J. P. SARTRE

Hell hath no music like a woman playing second fiddle.

JOHN PATRICK

If there is a paradise, there are many natures who will always worry whether they ought not to be somewhere else.

HENRY GREEN

To worship ourselves is to worship nothing. And the worship of nothing is hell.

THOMAS MERTON

'What worries me,' said a Yorkshireman to his friend, 'is that when I pass over to 'the other side' I don't know how I'll be able to draw my shirt down over my wings.'

'Nay, lad,' said his friend, 'Tha need not worry thysen abaht *that*. What tha *should* worry abaht is how to pull thy trousers up over thy tail!'

*   *   *

A man died, and woke up in what seemed to him very pleasant and familiar surroundings.

'I had no idea,' he said to a man who was sitting near him, 'that Heaven was so like Chicago.'

'But,' said his neighbour, 'you are not *in* Heaven.'

*   *   *

A clergyman had called to see a man who had been a pigeon-flying enthusiast and who was very seriously ill. After some talk about his hobby, the parson directed the conversation into a more serious channel and thought it no harm to tell the man that when he reached the Better Land he would have wings and be able to fly about himself.

'And will you have wings too?' asked the man.

The parson said that he hoped he would.

The man meditated for a moment, and then said: 'Well, 'appen we'll meet, and if we do ah'll fly thee for a fiver!'

*   *   *

Heaven
. . . 'a state in which nothing is impeding our complete activity and the full articulation of everything we are.'

HONOURS

*

The late George Senior, an Alderman of the Sheffield
City Council, who had contributed greatly to the social
services of his native city, was invited to attend the Royal
Garden Party. When he returned, his friends were chaffing
him in the 'local' where he used to have a drink in the
evening.

'Didn't King give thee a Knighthood, George?' they
asked.

'Well,' said the Alderman, 'I'll tell you wot 'appened.
T'King took me on one side an' sed: 'George,' 'e said, 'I've
watched wot tha's been an' done for Sheffield, an' I'd like
to give thee a Knighthood. I think tha's deserved it. But,
to tell thee t'honest truth, lad, I can't stand thy pals!'

*

A sinecure is a job with a portfolio and pay and no work. In a sense Henry VIII was a sinecure King.

* * *

Question: What do you know of Solomon?
Answer: He was very fond of animals because he had three hundred porcupines.

* * *

An epistle is the wife of an apostle.

* * *

Salome was a very wicked woman who wore very few clothes and took them all off when she danced before Harrods.

* * *

Question: What did the Israelites do when they came out of the Red Sea?
Answer: They dried themselves.

* * *

A limited Monarchy is a government by a monarch who, in case of a bankruptcy, would not be entirely responsible for the National Debt. You have the same thing in private life with a Limited Liability Company.

* * *

Describing the incident of Sir Walter Raleigh laying down his cloak, a boy wrote:

'Her Majesty remarked to Sir Walter: 'I am afraid I have spoiled your cloak,' to which the gallant knight replied, 'Dieu et mon droit,' which means, 'My God, and you're right.'

*   *   *

Members of Parliament are mostly business men. This is necessary, otherwise they couldn't earn a living.

*   *   *

The principal thing which was left behind by the Egyptians was their bones.

*   *   *

The death of Julius Caesar was foretold by a shower of metaphors.

*   *   *

Henry VIII was very cruel to Ann Boleyn and ironed her. (Text book reading: 'He pressed his suit on her.')

*   *   *

Question: Write a sentence showing clearly the meaning of 'posterity'.

Answer: 1. The man looked as if he had been reduced to posterity.

2. Henry pade the fare because of his posterity.

3. The cat leaped about and then sat on its posterity.

*   *   *

Shakespeare married Anne Hathaway, but he mostly lived at Windsor with his merry wives. This is quite usual with actors.

*   *   *

Question: What is a Pretender? Write a few lines about the Pretenders who have appeared in British History.

Answer: A 'pretender' is someone who thinks he can do two things at once, but he can't. Alfred the Great was a Pretender, because he pretended to look after the cakes and think of his enemies at the same time.

* * *

Many famous men have given their names to public convenience such as Hansom, Wellington, Blanket and Cascara.

* * *

Luther was a good and a great man, but after a diet of worms he said: 'So help me, God, I can take no other course!'

* * *

Question: What proof have we from the Scriptures that it is not lawful to have more than one wife?

Answer: The Bible says no man can serve two masters.

* * *

In most villages oil-lamps have been superimposed by electricity. When it is used for cooking it is called the Grid System.

* * *

Abraham had two wives. He kept one at home and he turned the other into a pillar of salt by day and a pillar of fire by night.

* * *

Queen Elizabeth was sometimes called a virgin, but only behind her back.

* * *

Psychology: The Oedipus Complex means liking your mother as if she were a normal woman.

*　　*　　*

'Where the bee sucks, there suck I' means, as far as I can see, that Shakespeare was fond of honey too.

*　　*　　*

The Matterhorn was a horn blown by the ancients when anything was the matter.

*　　*　　*

From examination paper of Student Nurses.

The eye is the organ of site, the site of which is in a holler in the temple.

At the back of the eye one may see a retinue.

The heart is a muscular organ acting like a human pump, which pumps the heart around the body at regular intervals.

The shopkeeper should thoroughly rap all cakes before selling them to make sure all disease is eliminated.

Food should not be picked up by the hand but with tongues.

Food should be kept covered in shops because of the diseased types who buy it.

The severity of an attack of coronary thrombosis depends on the sight of the clot.

British Medical Journal

*

ad nauseam—a disgusting poster.
pas de deux—father of twins.

*   *   *

Bearer bonds are investments given to women who ought to have children, generally by a man.

*   *   *

JOURNALISM

*

Journalism consists largely in saying 'Lord Jones died' to people who never knew that Lord Jones was alive.

G. K. CHESTERTON

The editorial 'we' has often been fatal to rising genius; though all the world knows that it is only a form of speech; very often employed by a single needy blockhead.

THOMAS BABINGTON MACAULAY

'Is there any news?'
'Not a new!'

*   *   *

There are a few newspapers in which you don't read between the lines—you read between the sheets.

Anon.

It is part of the social mission of every great newspaper to provide a refuge and a home for the largest possible number of salaried eccentrics.

MR ROY THOMPSON

KISSING

*

Kissing don't last; cookery do.
GEORGE MEREDITH

A man snatches the first kiss, pleads for the second, demands the third, takes the fourth, accepts the fifth—and endures all the rest.
HELEN ROWLAND

Marriage is the miracle that transforms a kiss from a pleasure into a duty. . . .
ibid

If you are ever in doubt as to whether or not you should kiss a pretty girl, always give her the benefit of the doubt.
THOMAS CARLYLE

A kiss is a pleasant reminder that two heads are better than one.
Anon.

. . . seal with a righteous Kiss
A dateless bargain to engrossing Death.
WILLIAM SHAKESPEARE

He parted his moustache and sought her lips.
Sentence from an imaginary Victorian novel

LAUGHTER

*

It is much easier to be good when living with people who laugh, than with those who always notice when the wind is in the east.

Anon.

Laughter has something in it in common with the ancient winds of faith and inspiration; it unfreezes pride and unwinds secrecy; it makes men forget themselves in the presence of something greater than themselves; something (as the common phrase goes about a joke) that they cannot resist.

G. K. CHESTERTON

A sense of humour is what makes you laugh at something which would make you mad if it happened to *you*.

Anon.

Laughter is the corrective force which prevents us from becoming cranks.

HENRI BERGSON

A good laugh is sunshine in the house

Anon.

Crosland had remarked at one point : 'I am anxious that the jury should not be confused.'

'The jury can take care of themselves,' said Smith sharply.

'I daresay they can,' said Crosland, 'but I want them to take care of me.'

There was loud laughter in which the judge and jury joined.

THE EARL OF BIRKENHEAD

The vulgar only laugh, but never smile; whereas well-bred people often smile, but seldom laugh.

LORD CHESTERFIELD

Perhaps I know best why it is man alone who laughs; he alone suffers so deeply that he had to invent laughter.

NIETZSCHE

If we consider the frequent reliefs we receive from laughter, and how often it breaks the gloom which is apt to depress the mind, one would take care not to grow too wise for so great a pleasure of life.

JOSEPH ADDISON

THE LAW

*

Between two girls, which hath the merriest eye,
I have perhaps some shallow spirit of judgment;
But in these nice sharp quillets of the law,
Good faith, I am no wiser than a daw.
>   WARWICK (the King-Maker)

He is no lawyer that cannot take two sides.
>   CHARLES LAMB

You cannot live without lawyers, and certainly you
cannot die without them.
>   JOSEPH H. CHOATE

Always remember that when you go into an attorney s
office door, you will have to pay for it, first or last.
>   ANTHONY TROLLOPE

If you laid all our laws end to end, there would *be* no
end.
>   ARTHUR BAER

It is impossible to tell where the law stops and justice
begins.   *ibid*

A countryman between two lawyers is like a fish between
two cats.
>   BENJAMIN FRANKLIN

Judge (interrupting Counsel, who was expounding an
elementary point of law in an appeal case): 'Mr ——, do
you not credit this court with a knowledge of the very
rudiments of law?'

Counsel: 'That, m'lud, was the mistake I made in the lower court.'

*　　　*　　　*

An Irish barrister of the Victorian era had a stock peroration which he used in his address to the jury, irrespective of the nature of the case which was being heard. It went something like this:

'Members of the jury, the great King Nebuchadnezzar saw inscribed on the mighty walls of Babylon these pregnant and fateful words: 'Mene, Mene, Tekel, Upharsin,' which being interpreted mean—'

The Judge interrupted testily: 'King Nebuchadnezzar saw no such words on the walls of Babylon—'

'M'lud,' said Counsel imperturbably, *'some* King certainly saw those words on *some* wall *somewhere,* and, whoever the King and wherever the wall, *the principle is the same!'*

*　　　*　　　*

Defending Counsel had agreed that his client had a dual personality. On passing sentence, the Judge remarked: 'Counsel has argued eloquently on your behalf that you are really two people, one very good and one very bad. As to that all I can say is that both of you must go to prison.'

*　　　*　　　*

Magistrate (to husband): 'Are you going to act as your wife's counsel in this case?'

Husband: 'I am no counsel—I only speak the truth.'

*　　　*　　　*

I was never ruined but twice: once when I lost a lawsuit, and once when I won one.

VOLTAIRE

When a barrister nervously began his speech for his client, a man named Tickle, with the words: 'Tickle—my client—the defendant, my lord,' the judge, Lord Kames, interrupted him by saying: 'Tickle him yourself, Harry; you are as able to do it as I am.'

*   *   *

Lawyer: A man who induces two other men to strip for a fight—and then runs off with their clothes.

A judge is a law student who marks his own examination papers.

H. L. MENCKEN

The one great principle of the English law is to make business for itself.

CHARLES DICKENS

A lawyer is a gentleman who rescues your estate from your enemies and keeps it to himself.

LORD BROUGHAM

Solicitor A to Solicitor B: 'Sir, I regret to inform you that there is a danger of agreement breaking out between our respective clients.'

That is no mere imagined jibe (in cases relating to separation or divorce). It is what often vexatiously happens.

REGINALD L. HINE

The more I see of litigation, the more determined I am to keep out of it myself.

HIS HONOUR J. TUDOR REES

Counsel (cross-examining): 'All right then; now you're after saying so-and-so, and (*fortissimo*) five minutes before you said so-and-so. What do you mean by that? Have you no respect for the truth at all?'

The harassed witness turned to him, furious at the trap into which he now saw he had been led.

'I have too much respect for it,' he declared, 'than to be dragging it out before the likes of yourself.'

SIR CHRISTOPHER LYNCH-ROBINSON

The trouble with law is lawyers.

CLARENCE DARROW

A successful lawsuit is one worn by a policeman.

ROBERT FROST

John Clerk (afterwards Lord Eldon) was arguing a Scotch appeal case before the House of Lords. His client claimed the use of a mill-stream by prescriptive right.

Mr Clerk spoke broad Scotch, and argued that 'the watter had rin that way for forty years. Indeed naebody kenned how long, and why should his client now be deprived of the watter?'

The Lord Chancellor, amused at Clerk's pronunciation, asked him in a rather bantering tone: 'Mr Clerk, do you spell water in Scotland with two t's?'

Clerk, nettled at this hit at his natural tongue, answered:

'Na, my lord, we dinna spell *watter* wi' two t's, but we *do* spell *mainners* wi' two n's.'

*   *   *

Castles in the air are the only property you can own without the intervention of lawyers. Unfortunately, however, there are no title deeds to them.

HIS HONOUR J. TUDOR REES

I think we may class lawyers in the natural history of monsters.

KEATS

Of the professions, it may be said that soldiers are becoming too popular, parsons too lazy, physicians too mercenary, and lawyers too powerful.

C. C. CALTON (in 1820)

A friend of the Victorian Lord Salisbury was arguing that a Bishop had more power than a Judge.

'A Judge can only say "You be hanged", whereas a Bishop can say : "You be damned".'

'Yes,' said Lord Salisbury, 'but when a Judge says "You be hanged", you *are* hanged.'

*　　*　　*

I suppose they'll give you the custody of the Daimler?

NOEL COWARD

Judge Willis, a County Court Judge, after a long wrangle with Mr F. E. Smith upon a point of procedure, asked plaintively : 'What do you think I am on the Bench for, Mr Smith?'

'It is not for me, Your Honour, to attempt to fathom the inscrutable workings of Providence.'

THE EARL OF BIRKENHEAD

MANAGEMENT

*

Healthy self-criticism and an abiding willingness to learn seem to me to be the most important requirements of any manager.   THE DUKE OF EDINBURGH

Industrial Psychology : The technique of scientific selection is something like this :

(a) You take your candidate and place before him an unfamiliar piece of prose. If he can read it he isn't blind. If he can't read it he is either blind or can't read, in either of which cases he is unsuitable.

(b) If he gets through this test satisfactorily, you take him along, place him in front of a machine, and tell him to look at it. If, when you come back an hour later he is still looking at it, he is suitable. If, on the other hand, he has stopped looking at it, note what he has begun to do. The following list shows how this may help you to fit him into an appropriate job.

If he is	Then he is more suitable for
Asleep	Night-Watchman
Gone	Traveller
Reading the paper	Director
Writing a letter	Clerical post
Looking at the girl on next machine	Personel department
Arguing with somebody	Accountant
Looking at his watch	Time Study
Contemplating	Monk or Director

The main idea is to place people in positions where they may use their natural bent. If people have no natural bent, but just stay straight all the time, they are suitable as Cashiers.

From *How to run a Bassoon Factory*
by Mark Spade

MARRIAGE

*

Marriage is an institution the appreciation of which increases as one grows older.

SIR THOMAS BEECHAM

I gravely doubt whether women were ever married by capture. I think they pretended to be; as they do still.

G. K. CHESTERTON

I dislike the idea of wives about a house: they accumullate dust. Besides, so few of the really nice women in my set could afford to marry me.

SAKI

Marriage is like a beleaguered fortress, those who are without want to get in, and those within to get out.

QUITARD

Marry, or marry not—you will always regret it.

*   *   *

Being a husband is a whole-time job. That is why so many husbands fail. They cannot give their entire attention to it.

ARNOLD BENNETT

It's a great mistake, I do believe,
For married people to take anything for granted.

T. S. ELIOT

As regards marriage we are all, even the most knowing of us, in the lap of the Gods. The best we can hope for is that the Gods won't open their knees and drop us on the floor.

SIR SEYMOUR HICKS

Those who marry to escape something usually find something else.

GEORGE ADE

He had heard that one is permitted a certain latitude with widows and went in for the whole 180 degrees.

ibid

The happiness of a married man depends on the people he has not married. OSCAR WILDE

Bachelors know more about women than married men; if they didn't, they'd be married too.

H. L. MENCKEN

Love is like war : easy to begin but very hard to stop.

ibid

Very few people can afford to marry their first loves.

Anon.

All women criticize the woman who marries a man much younger than herself, but, given the opportunity, which of her critics would not emulate her?

Anon.

It is no excuse when you are neglecting your wife to say it doesn't matter because she is only a relation by marriage. SIR SEYMOUR HICKS

Young wife : 'I've been trying to figure out where my husband spends his evenings. Last night I came home early —and there he was.'

*   *   *

Some one asked Sydney Smith whether a certain Bishop was going to get married.

'Perhaps he may,' was the answer, 'yet how can a Bishop marry? How can he flirt? The most he can say is, 'I will see you in the vestry after service.'

* * *

'Do you think I'm too young to marry, Aunt?'

'If I had my time again, dear,' replied the old maid, 'I'd get married before I had sense enough not to.'

* * *

There be three things that drive the good man from home, to wit, a dripping roof, a smoking chimney and a scolding woman. Wherefore, fair sister, I pray you that in order to keep yourself in love and good favour with your husband you be unto him gentle, amiable and debonair.   *The Ménagier of Paris*

When an acquaintance was described as having been 'egged on' to matrimony, Dr Leigh observed: 'Let us hope the yoke will sit lightly on him.'

ELIZABETH JENKINS

'Tell me,' said the newly-married man to his oldest friend, 'just what do you think of my wife? I know I can rely on you to give me your unbiased opinion.'

'Well,' said his friend, 'if you would really like to know, I don't like her.'

'Neither do I,' said the husband.

* * *

A man had been introduced to a woman through the agency of an Introduction Club 'for marriage, friendship and holidays.'

'Madam,' he said, 'I am a lonely man and I desire companionship, but I cannot suggest marriage, for three reasons. First, because I have no money . . .'

She said: 'You need not trouble to enumerate the other two.'

*   *   *

'Men are what women marry. They drink and smoke and swear, but do not go to church. Perhaps if they wore bonnets they would. They are more logical than women and also more zoological. Both men and women spring from monkeys, but the women spring further than the men.'

From a schoolgirl's essay.

Wife (to husband): 'You're lazy, you're worthless, you're bad-tempered, you're shiftless, you're a thorough liar.'

Husband (reasonably): 'Well, my dear, no man is perfect.'

*   *   *

Christian men are accustomed to be content with one wife, and even in America with one at a time.

RONALD KNOX

Between a woman's 'yes' and 'no', I would not venture to stick a pin.

CERVANTES

It is specially important that the wife of a public man should efface herself—not to the public but to him. *He* needs all the room there is in matrimony.

Anon.

'My wife's a wonder,' boasted a proud husband. 'One winter she knitted me socks out of an old bathing suit, and now she's knitting herself a bathing suit out of one of my old socks.

*   *   *

'If you were to say to my wife that a lot of water had flowed under the bridge since we first met, she'd say: "*What* bridge?"'

* * *

Think of your ancestors and your posterity, and you will never marry. ETHEL WATTS MUMFORD

The great necessity in life is at all costs to go on loving.
Anon.

The prudent husband leaves diplomacy till dinner.
Anon.

A life-long devotion should never last less than two years; by that time it will have seemed life-long. *Anon.*

Marriage is popular because it combines the maximum of temptation with the maximum of opportunity.
GEORGE BERNARD SHAW

'I don't know, Smith,' said his next door neighbour, 'why it is that everyone seems to have the impression that your wife keeps you under her thumb; in short, that you are thoroughly henpecked. Why, last night I heard you reproving your wife bitterly.'
'Well, wouldn't you, old man,' asked Smith, 'when she dropped her cigarette ash on the floor I had just washed?'
The Dalesman

Marriage is all very well, but it isn't romance; there's nothing wrong in it. *ibid*

After a few years of marriage, a man can look right at a woman without seeing her—and a woman can see right through a man without looking at him.

HELEN ROWLAND

Woman at Highgate Police Court: 'My husband won't allow discussion on any subject. He says his say, then he gives a grunt and says: "I have spoken." '

A man who had been married twice and lost both wives, married a third time a woman whose first step was to clear the cupboards and drawers out.

Coming across two hats (in a drawer) wrapped up in tissue paper, she inquired of her husband what they were there for.

'They belonged ter mi other wives,' he explained, 'and they looked so nice in 'em Ah thowt Ah'd keep 'em.'

'Well,' replied she, 'they're going on t'fire, and understand, t'next 'at that'll be kept in 'ere'll be a *bowler*.'

The Dalesman

Marriage: the state or condition of a community consisting of a master, a mistress, and two slaves, making in all two.

AMBROSE BIERCE

Marriage is the miracle that transforms a kiss from a pleasure into a duty, and a life from a luxury into a necessity.   *ibid*

Before marriage a man will lie awake all night thinking about something you said; after marriage he'll fall asleep before you finish saying it.

HELEN ROWLAND

Every man wants a woman to appeal to his better side, his nobler instincts and his higher nature—and another woman to help him forget them.

ibid

Being married to a sleepy-souled woman is just like playing at cards for nothing; no passion is excited, and the time is filled up.   DR JOHNSON

Marriage is hardly a thing one can do now and then—except in America.

OSCAR WILDE

A good marriage is that in which each appoints the other guardian of his solitude.

RAINER MARIA RILKE

A wife encourages her husband's vices in order to excuse her own.

RUSSELL GREEN

Polygamy over-simplifies one's emotional life, while monogamy over-complicates it.

ibid

The materialism of a wife forms a valuable corrective to the idealism of a husband. *ibid*

The surest hit with men is a near-Miss.

ibid

Husbands have only themselves to blame for the discovery of wives.

ibid

Marriage, which makes two one, is a lifelong struggle to discover which is that one.

Anon.

A man can't argue with the woman he loves.

Anon.

'And what words would you like on your tombstone, my sweet?' asked a husband, trying a rather macabre method of rousing his wife from a fit of hypochondria. 'Wife of the above,' she replied promptly. The ruse had succeeded.

* * *

Dr Johnson was asked by Mrs Piozzi if he ever disputed with his wife.

'Perpetually,' he said; 'my wife had a particular reverence for cleanliness, and desired the praise of neatness in her dress and furniture, as many ladies do, till they become troublesome to their best friends, slaves to their own besoms, and only sigh for the hour of sweeping their husbands out of the house as dirt and useless lumber.'

* * *

The hostess poured a cup of tea for a middle-aged man at her party and asked him if he took sugar.

'No,' he said.

'Yes,' said his wife brightly at the same moment. Then she turned accusingly to him. 'But I *always* put sugar in your tea!'

'I know,' the man said ruefully. 'I used to remind you not to. Now I just don't stir.'

Readers Digest

Nobody enjoys a wedding but the bride's mother—she likes a good cry.

R. W. KAUFFMAN

Small boy (to his mother, after attending a wedding): 'Mummy, is it now he puts the pollen on?'

* * *

Husband (to his wife, after the wedding): 'Don't think of it as losing a daughter; think of it as gaining a bathroom.'

* * *

'Tell me, Tom, who is the boss in your house?'

'Well,' Tom answered thoughtfully, 'Margie assumes command of the children, the servants, the dog and the parakeet. But I say pretty much what I please to the gold-fish.'

*   *   *

Fortune teller: 'Do you want to know something about your future husband, Madam?'

Client: 'No, I want to know something about the past of my present husband for my future use.'

MEN AND WOMEN

*

Mellefont: 'Shall we go to the ladies, my lord?'
Lord Froth: 'With all my heart, methinks we are a
solitude without 'em.'

WILLIAM CONGREVE

Men have a much better time of it than women; for one
thing, they marry later; for another thing they die earlier.

H. L. MENCKEN

If you really wish to know a woman's bad points—praise
her to another.

Anon.

Actress (to friend): 'Have you met my husband?'
Friend: 'I'm always glad to meet any husband of yours.

*　　*　　*

Incompatability between husband and wife tends to
become acute when he has no income and she is no longer
pattable.　　　　　　　　　　　　　　*Anon.*

*　　*　　*

Woman's Voice: 'There, my dear, you must be tired
after your long's day's work at the office. Sit down in your
armchair. There are your slippers, and here's your pipe.'

Man's Voice: 'Good Lord! I'm in the wrong house!'
From a BBC Kenneth Horne Programme

The lives of great men rarely remind us of anything
sublime.　　　　　　　　　　LORD VANSITTART

MONEY

*

The more a man possesses over and above what he uses the more careworn he becomes.

GEORGE BERNARD SHAW

'Pay as you earn' is the Inland Revenue's retort to 'Music while you work'.

RUSSELL GREEN

Money's all right, but you can waste a powerful lot of time making it.

Anon.

A man was asked if he lived within his income. 'Certainly not,' he replied. 'It takes me all my time to live within my credit.'

* * *

'We need more money,' said the vicar, 'for our organ repair fund—and if we can't get it by fair means, we'll have to organize another sale of work.'

* * *

'When I started to work,' said the business executive, 'I used to dream about getting the salary I'm now starving on.'

* * *

No one makes money like the man who invents our fads.

Anon.

There's nothing so comfortable as a small bankroll. A big one is always in danger.

WILSON MIZNER

There is only one class in the community that thinks more about money than the rich, and that is the poor.

OSCAR WILDE

Economy is a method of spending money without extracting from it the slightest degree of pleasure.

*   *   *

Lack of money is the root of all evil.

GEORGE BERNARD SHAW

When a man begins to think seriously of saving for a rainy day, it's probably a rainy day.

*   *   *

The narrowing of the differential between the letter rate and the postcard rate strikes me as an unholy procedure. I used to save 50 per cent by despatching a postcard; now I save only 16.2/3 per cent. Has my salary been adjusted accordingly? No.

GEORGE SCHWARTZ

I have been very poor the greater part of my life and have borne it as well, I think, as most people; but I can safely say that I have been happier every guinea I have gained.

SYDNEY SMITH

It's better to give than to lend—and it costs about the same.

SIR PHILIP GIBBS

'Poverty needs a good time,' they say, and a very good proverb too. Most people are poor and it is quite bearable provided every now and then you can lose your head and throw everything to the winds.

PETER MAYNE

Money isn't everything—but it's a long way ahead of what comes next.

SIR EDMUND STOCKDALE
(Lord Mayor of London, 1959-60)

God shows his contempt for wealth by the kind of person He selects to receive it.

AUSTIN O'MALLEY

Harried wife to husband and children: 'Well, I worked out a budget. But one of us will have to go.'

*   *   *

Man who received by mistake a pay envelope without a cheque, to accounting department: 'What happened? Did my deductions finally catch up with my salary?'

*   *   *

Overheard: I hope they don't raise the standard of living any higher. I can't afford it now.'

MAT WEINSTOCK

The best things in life are free, of course;—but isn't it a pity that so many of the *next best* things are so expensive?'

Anon.

Taking it all in all, I find it is more trouble to watch after money than to get it.

MONTAIGNE

It is only by not paying one's bills that one can hope to live in the memory of the commercial classes.

OSCAR WILDE

The elegant simplicity of the three per cents.

LORD STOWELL

Money speaks sense in a language all nations understand.

ALFRED BEHAN

The money that men make lives after them.

SAMUEL BUTLER

It saves a lot of trouble if, instead of having to earn money and save it, you can just go and borrow it.

SIR WINSTON CHURCHILL

It is a socialist idea that making profits is a vice; I consider the real vice is making losses.

ibid

Money often costs too much.

RALPH WALDO EMERSON

When a man has had to work so hard to get money, why should he impose on himself the further hardship of trying to save it?

DON HEROLD

The gentle are of spending money requires neither a correspondence course nor an instructor.

Anon.

A lady was notified by her banker that her account was overdrawn, and promptly drew a cheque for the amount of the overdraft and sent it to him.

* * *

An American woman telephoned her bank manager and asked him to dispose of a thousand-dollar bond.

'Is the bond for redemption or conversion?' asked the Bank Manager.

There was a pause, and then the woman asked: 'Am I talking to the First National Bank, or the First Baptist Church?'

*   *   *

Not that we ever had any money: but any fool knows that you don't need money to get enjoyment out of life.
                                          THOMAS MERTON

Speculate when you have more money than you need; not when you need more money than you have.

*   *   *

Wife (to husband holding a large batch of cancelled cheques in his hand):

'You mean the bank saves all the cheques I write and sends them to you? What an underhand thing to do!'

*   *   *

Some day a tax return may contain only three questions:

    1. How much money have you got?
    2. Where is it?
    3. How soon can you get at it?

*   *   *

A North Yorkshire roadman won quite a substantial prize in a raffle. Yet his friends were surprised that instead of being pleased he was very gloomy about it.

'Why, Kit, what's the matter?' asked a pal.

'Nay,' he said. 'Thoo see Ah've wasted gooid money on t'other ticket. Why Aw ever bought two beats me?'

*   *   *

In the bad old days . . . there were three easy ways of losing money—racing being the quickest, women the pleasantest and farming the most certain.

LORD AMHERST OF HACKNEY

I have every contempt for what money does to people. If you haven't got it, it knocks hell out of you, and if you have, it does, too.

WILLIAM SAROYAN

The atmosphere reeked of the delicious odour of un-earned money.

PETER BLACK

The village grocer speedily summed up the new vicar: 'Parson be a proper gentleman. He don't know the price of nothing.'

GEORGE SCHWARTZ

The road surveyor wrote to the Town Clerk stating that his men needed more spades. He received this reply.
'Retrenchment demanded by the council makes it impossible to authorize further expenditure on spades. Tell the men to lean on one another.'

On his first Sunday at a country church a new vicar was shocked to see the clerk take half-a-crown out of the alms dish, and gave him a strong rebuke.
'Why,' said the clerk, 'whatever are you talking about? I've led off with that half-crown for the last twenty years.'

Motor accident : A head-on collision between two stationary cars parked on their own sides of the road.

Parking Space : An unfillable opening in an unending line of cars near an unapproachable fire plug.

*   *   *

A motorist drew in to the curb on a signal from a policeman, who asked to see his driving licence.

'But,' he protested, 'I wasn't doing anything wrong.'

'I know,' said the constable, 'but you were driving so carefully that I thought maybe you didn't have your licence with you.'

*   *   *

Before our highways became choked with motor vehicles it was good to be alive; today it is a surprise.

HIS HONOUR J. TUDOR REES

Leisured persons who own cars seem to be in a state of perpetual flight from one place to another, in the endeavour to escape from something unpleasant which is waiting to pounce on them at whatever place they happen to be. On no other assumption is the behaviour of those motoring for pleasure explicable.   C. E. M. JOAD

Guest (on leaving his host's house and dining very well indeed) :

'Is that my car on the left or the right?'

Footman : 'On the left, sir. The car on the right is a subjective phenomenon.'

*   *   *

Five hundred brand-new motor cars each morning rode
  the roads,
And flashed about like comets or sat motionless as toads,
Whichever course they took they made the public high-
  way hell,
And everybody wondered why the population fell.

SIR ALAN HERBERT

Motorist (to his companion in a car): 'I think that we are
getting nearer town now.'

Companion: 'What makes you think that?'

Motorist: 'Well, we seem to be hitting more people.'

*   *   *

A schoolboy was asked what was the difference between
the Quick and the Dead.

'Well,' he said, 'the Quick are those who get out of the
way in time; the Dead are those who don't.'

*   *   *

A woman driver was pulled up at the traffic lights by a
policeman, who asked her to drive into the kerb.

'May I see your driving licence, madam?' he asked.

'I haven't got one,' she told him.

'But you must have one, madam,' he insisted.

'Don't be silly,' she said. 'How could I have one when
they took it away from me last Spring?'

*   *   *

The difference between the driver of a new car and the
owner of a new car is about twenty-four monthly pay-
ments.

Two Yorkshire country magistrates were summoned for
exceeding the speed limit in a built-up area. When they

arrived at the court there were no other magistrates present, so they agreed to try each other. No. 1 went on the bench and No. 2 in the witness box. A question was asked: 'You are charged with exceeding the speed limit. Do you plead guilty or not guilty?' 'Guilty, your worship.' 'You will be fined five shillings.'

They then changed places and No. 2 went on the bench. He said to No. 1: 'You are charged with exceeding the speed limit in a built-up area. Do you plead guilty or not guilty?' 'Guilty, your worship. 'Now, these speed cases are becoming far too common. This is the second we have had this morning. You will be fined thirty shillings.'

The Dalesman

If you give a woman an inch she'll park a car in it.
The Chief Constable of Gloucestershire

Anybody seeing the accident keep quiet—as the driver was a policeman.

From *The Goon Show*

PAINTING

*

Every time I paint a portrait I lose a friend.
J. S. SARGENT

Modern paintings are full of protoplasmic blobs.
HUMBERT WOLFE

'Is thy servant a dog, that he should do this thing?'
SYDNEY SMITH
(When advised to have his portrait
painted by Landseer)

'Yes, Madam, Nature is creeping up!'
J. M. WHISTLER
(to a lady who said that a landscape
reminded her of his work)

Only the artist who has married for love can appreciate the necessity of remaining single for art.
RUSSELL GREEN

It is only an auctioneer who should admire all schools of art.
OSCAR WILDE

'. . . Talking about the death of surrealism to those who didn't know it had been alive.
Anon.

It's wonderful; I must make a resolution to work only in the open air. I have a strong suspicion that all the pictures of the old masters showing outdoor scenes are artificial; they don't seem to have the true and, above all, the perpetually near appearance of nature itself.
CEZANNE

I do not paint a portrait to look like the subject, rather does the person grow to look like his portrait.

SALVADOR DALI

In painting the gravest immorality is to try to finish what isn't well begun. But a picture that is well begun may be left off at any point. Look at Cézanne's water-colours . . .

MATHEW SMITH

I'm painting now with the rapture of a *Marseillais* eating bouillabaisse, which won't surprise you when you hear that the subject is big sunflowers.

VINCENT VAN GOGH
(in a letter to his brother Theo)

PARTIES

*

The best parties are given by people who can't afford them.

ELSA MAXWELL

It was one of those parties where you cough twice before you speak, and then decide not to say it after all.

P. G. WODEHOUSE

Mother (to her son, leaving home to go to a party):
'You'll be a good boy, won't you, dear?'
Boy: 'Yes, Mother, what shall I not do?'

*   *   *

'I hope I don't protrude,' said the foreign gentleman, joining the company uninvited.

*   *   *

At an evening party an artist who had lately been charged with an attempt upon the virtue of a servant entered leaning upon a stick. A lady asked Steer what was wrong with the new arrival. 'Housemaid's Knee,' he replied.

*   *   *

'PASS THE MILK' (a few 'catty' remarks)

*

. . . but, egad, I love to be malicious. Nay, deuce take me, there's wit in't too.   WILLIAM CONGREVE

They say she is not ugly, and has as good a set of teeth as one can have, when one has but two and those black.
                                                 HORACE WALPOLE
(On the daughter-in-law of the Spanish Ambassador)

Her features did not seem to know the value of team-work.   GEORGE ADE

He had the sort of face that, once seen, is never remembered.   OSCAR WILDE

He has not an enemy in the world, and none of his friends like him.   OSCAR WILDE (of Bernard Shaw)

Frank Harris is invited to all the great houses in England —once.   OSCAR WILDE

She was a town-and-country soprano of the kind often used for augmenting the grief at funerals.
                                                 GEORGE ADE

With Macaulay it was difficult to 'get a word in edge-ways'. Sydney Smith once said to him: 'Now, Macaulay, when I am gone you'll be sorry you never heard me speak.' On another occasion he said that he found Macaulay in bed from illness, and that he was therefore more agreeable than he had ever seen him: 'There were some glorious flashes of silence.'

*   *   *

'What do you think of the violinist?' George Bernard Shaw was once asked by his hostess at a music party.

'He reminds me of Paderewski,' replied Shaw.

'But Paderewski is not a violinist.'

'Neither is this gentleman.'

*   *   *

The hero of his heart was Stonewall Jackson, and he based his life upon the shibboleths of famous generals, most of which seemed to me to have been uttered when under the influence of drink.

SIR CHRISTOPHER LYNCH-ROBINSON, BART.

She ran the whole gamut of emotions from A to B.

DOROTHY PARKER

She was a professional athlete—of the tongue.

ALDOUS HUXLEY

In America the young are always ready to give to those who are older the full benefits of their inexperience.

OSCAR WILDE

Her face was her chaperone.

RUPERT HUGHES

Boys will be boys, and so will a lot of middle-aged men.

F. M. HUBBARD

All the time that he can spare from the adornment of his person he devotes to the neglect of his duties.

PROFESSOR SIDGWICK
(of Sir Richard Jebb)

It really deserves the praise, whatever that praise may be worth, of being the best book ever written by any man on the wrong side of the question of which he was profoundly ignorant.

THOMAS BABINGTON MACAULAY

It is a pity he has not a little law for then he would have something of everything.

DANIEL O'CONNELL
(when the versatile Brougham
became Lord Chancellor)

His eminence was due to the flatness of the surrounding landscape.

(Said by a German of John Stuart Mill)

He discloses the workings of a mind to which incoherence lends an illusion of profundity.

T. DE VERE WHITE (of De Valera)

Your manuscript is both good and original; but the part that is good is not original, and the part that is original is not good.

DR JOHNSON

"On 'Blue Streak' and the saving of Mr Duncan Sandys' face): 'This is the most expensive face in history, certainly since that of Helen launched 1,000 ships, and at any rate they were operational!"

MR HAROLD WILSON, MP

One young girl to another: 'Sylvia is one of those sweet, shy, unassuming girls. You know, a real phoney.'

'All self, yet he had so little self.'
W. B. YEATS (of George Moore)

'Well, his mind's never been raped by an idea.'
MARY McCARTHY (of Ernest Hemingway)

PHILOSOPHY

*

Experience is not what happens to a man; it is what a man does with what happens to him.

ALDOUS HUXLEY

The art of life is to get the credit of knowing more than one has ever learnt.

Anon.

Experience is the comb that Nature gives us when we are bald.

Belgian Proverb

Dignity is like a top hat. Neither is very much use when you are standing on it.

CHRISTOPHER HOLLIS

Cut the wings of your hopes and hens lest they lead you a weary dance after them..

BENJAMIN FRANKLIN

There is no cure for birth or death save to enjoy the interval.

GEORGE SANTAYANA

Broad-mindedness is the result of flattening high-mindedness out.

ibid

Fanaticism consists in redoubling your effort when you have forgotten your aim.

ibid

Life is not a spectacle or a feast; it is a punishment.

ibid

(*On French Philosophers*):
They think me quite profane for having any belief left.

HORACE WALPOLE

I think they are ten times more foolish since they took
to thinking.

ibid

. . . To sit down in a quiet ignorance of those things
which, upon examination, are found to be beyond the
range of our capacities.

LOCKE

To profit from good advice requires more wisdom than
to give it.

JOHN CHURTON COLLINS

A 'new thinker', when studied closely, is merely a man
who does not know what other people have thought.

FRANK MOORE COLBY

Society is composed of two great classes: those who
have more dinners than appetite, and those who have more
appetite than dinners.

NICHOLAS CHAMFORT

There is no record in human history of a happy
philosopher.

H. L. MENCKEN

If someone hadn't the courage to be stupid now and then,
the world would be a terribly dull place.

Anon.

If people look bad, they are; if they look good, they may
be.   *Anon.*

Everyone is as God made him—and very often worse.

A person who owns nothing can do nothing and be nothing.   SIR HENRY JONES

Some people have such open minds that nothing stays in them long.   HIS HONOUR J. TUDOR REES

An open mind is all very well in its way, but it ought not to be so open that there is no keeping anything in or out of it. It should be capable of shutting its doors sometimes, or it may be found a little draughty.

SAMUEL BUTLER

Making the best of it.
      There's one thing about baldness,—it's neat.
                                        DON HEROLD

There is no place for the philosopher in the modern world, except perhaps as a comedian in the Brains Trust.

*   *   *

Imagination is given to man to compensate him for what he is not; a sense of humour to console him for what he is.

*   *   *

What is mind? No matter. What is matter? Never mind.
                                        T. H. KEY

On the death of a German Philosopher.
            He wrote *The I and the It*
            He wrote *The It and the Me*
            He died at Marienbad
            And now we are all at sea.

STEVIE SMITH

130

For those who do not think, it is best at least to re-arrange their prejudices once in a while.

LUTHER BURBANK

A man can no more possess a private religion than he can possess a private sun and moon.

G. K. CHESTERTON

A foolish consistency is the hobgoblin of little minds.

T. W. EMERSON

Life is like playing a violin solo in public and learning the instrument as one goes on.

SAMUEL BUTLER

The way to love anything is to realize that it might be lost.

G. K. CHESTERTON

Many are called but few get up.

OLIVER HERFORD

The only great danger that exists is man himself.

DR. C. J. JUNG

It is better for the old man to look forward to the next day as if it were for centuries.

ibid

Man cannot stand a meaningless life.

ibid

Metaphysicians are musicians without musical ability.

RUDOLF CARNAP

Humility is the first of the virtues—for other people.

OLIVER WENDELL HOLMES

Heredity is an omnibus in which all our ancestors ride, and every now and then one of them puts his head out and embarrasses us.

ibid

It is a far, far better thing to have a firm anchor in nonsense than to put out in the troubled seas of thought.

PROFESSOR J. K. GALBRAITH

Philosophy consists largely of one philosopher arguing that all others are jackasses. He usually proves it, and I should add that he also usually proves that he is one himself.

H. L. MENCKEN

I have tried in my time to be a philosopher; but, I don't know how, cheerfulness was always breaking in.

OLIVER EDWARDS
(friend of Dr. Johnson)

If I wished to punish a province, I would have it governed by philosophers.

FREDERICK THE GREAT

If a man is only a little lower than the angels, the angels should reform.

MARY WILSON LITTLE

There are those who so dislike the nude that they find something indecent in the naked truth.

F. H. BRADLEY

Everything comes to him who waits—among other things—death.

ibid

There is no fun in having nothing to do; the fun is having lots to do and not doing it.   *ibid*

A highbrow is a man who has found something more interesting than women. EDGAR WALLACE

I shall be so polite to my wife as though she were a perfect stranger.

ROBERT JONES BURDETTE

Horse sense is what keeps a horse from betting on a man.

*   *   *

Word has somehow got around that the split infinitive is always wrong. This is of a piece with the outworn notion that it is always wrong to strike a lady.

ROBERT BENCHLEY

The optimist proclaims that we live in the best of all possible worlds, and the pessimist fears that this is true.

JAMES BRANCH CABELL

The greatest help to overcoming mistakes is to acknowledge them.

*   *   *

It is said that all things come to him who waits, but the fellow who goes after them gets the pick.

*   *   *

One of the advantages of telling the truth is that you need not remember what you said.

*   *   *

Diogenes was twitted that he pretended to be a philosopher and knew nothing: I am the greater Philosopher, said he, for Philosophy consists in making doubts of all things.

JOHN BALTUL

Pythagoras said that the whole world was a Comedy, of which the Philosophers were the spectators.

ibid

Habit may be likened to a cable; every day we weave a thread and soon we cannot break it.

Anon.

Nothing so needs reforming as other people's habits.

MARK TWAIN

We get our parents at so late an age that it is impossible to change their habits.

(From a schoolboy's essay)

The tragedy of life is not so much what men suffer but rather what they miss.

THOMAS CARLYLE

Love your neighbour—but don't pull down your hedge.

BENJAMIN FRANKLIN

Love lives on propinquity and dies of contact.

THOMAS HARDY

The truth is the one thing that nobody will believe.

GEORGE BERNARD SHAW

There are only two classes in good society in England: The equestrian classes and the neurotic classes.

ibid

I like Frenchmen very much, because even when they insult you they do it so nicely.

JOSEPHINE BAKER

The test of good manners is being able to put up with bad ones.

Anon.

Be nice to people on your way up because you'll meet them on your way down.

WILSON MIZNER

Overheard:

'Life is sweet, I suppose—anyway we ought to think so.'

Life is an experiment in the art of living, but you die before you see the result.

RUSSELL GREEN

The man I am sorry for is the man who goes through life without any *invisible* means of support..

HIS HONOUR J. TUDOR REES

He did not want to contemplate truth but to subjugate it.

NORMAN MALCOLM
(of Ludwig Wittgenstein)

I don't believe that there is somewhere a great wodge of something called Truth and that you can go and cut a piece of it for yourself.

SIR JOHN WOLFENDEN

We should expect the best and the worst from mankind, as from the weather.

VAAVENARGUES

He who draws upon his own resources easily comes to an end of his wealth.

WILLIAM HAZLITT

Don't do for others what you wouldn't think of asking them to do for you.

'JOSH BILLINGS'

Never argue at the dinner table, for the one who is not hungry always gets the best of the argument.

ARCHBISHOP WHATELY

A teenager who was soon to be confirmed asked her mother if she could send confirmation cards to some of her friends, who were to be confirmed at the same time.

'Confirmation cards? What are they?' her mother asked.

'Oh, they just say something like "Congratulations on your confirmation and best wishes for after-life!" '

*   *   *

We may speculate on worlds, we must act in families, in districts and in kingdoms.

SYDNEY SMITH

No wonder the men concerned* are half out of their minds, demand to have observation posts in outer space, would like to bring the Moon in on their side, inventing more and more monstrous excuses for the most extravagant antics in all men's history. I am not blaming them. If I had lived and worked as long as most of them have in a top-secret, top-priority, top-security, top-non-sense atmosphere, I might be even dafter than they are.

J. B. PRIESTLEY

The study of immortality is necessarily a long-term project.

DR S. A. PARKES, F.R.S.

He had, he said, studied the great philosophers and had therefore come to expect very little in this life, and rather less in the next.

ALEX ATKINSON

* with nuclear research.

POETRY

*

Poetry lifts the veil from the hidden beauty of the world.

P. B. SHELLEY

Angling is somewhat like poetry, men are to be born so.

IZAAK WALTON

I wish our clever young poets would remember my homely definitions of prose and poetry; that is, prose—words in their best order; poetry—the *best* words in the best order.

S. T. COLERIDGE

Language is simplified gesture, and poetry is simplified language. . . . Poetry is a sort of dancing with the voice.

FRANCIS SCARFE

I would rather be the author of that poem than take Quebec.

GENERAL WOLFE
(referring to Gray's 'Elegy' on the 13th September, 1759, just before the taking of Quebec)

A poet defies the public from the start, by the mere act of writing poetry.

Times Literary Supplement

A poet can survive anything but a misprint.

OSCAR WILDE

Books of poetry by young writers are usually promissory notes that are never met.

ibid

'A woman with such beautiful legs as yours should not worry her head about poetry.'

The poet Algernon Charles Swinburne to the
equestrienne Adan Dolores Menken

The Poetaster

> Rewrite the thrice rewritten. Strive to say
> Some older nothing in some newer way.
>
> J. ST. LOE STRACHEY

A Welsh miner asked Dylan Thomas what he did.
'I am a poet,' replied Dylan proudly.
'You have no right to be a poet,' said the miner, looking at him with astonishment. 'You have the face of a perfectly good Welsh miner.'

*   *   *

Poetry can console, enchant, ennoble; it can transfigure the world with the magic of moonlight; but its greatest lovers are seldom the most cheerful or practical of men.

F. L. LUCAS
(*The Art of Living*)

Poets are born, not paid.

ADDISON MIZNER

I've read some of your modern free verse and wonder who set it free.

JOHN BARRYMORE

The poet is a liar who always speaks the truth.

JEAN COCTEAU

I wonder how much the popularity of the nightingale among poets is due to its name rather than to its song.

Anon.

Someone said that he could only understand the first and the last line of Browning's long and obscure poem *Sordello*—and that they weren't true.

The first line is:

> 'Who will may hear Sordello's story told,'
>   and the last line is:
> 'Who would has heard Sordello's story told.'

*   *   *

POLITICS

*

Any government that is big enough to give you everything you want is big enough to take everything you've got.
Anon.

We all make the mistake of thinking about institutions, such as business and government, as ends in themselves.
ADLAI E. STEVENSON

Abraham Lincoln's famous 'of, by, and for the people' is good rhetoric, but a system of government cannot be built on a foundation of prepositions.
PROFESSOR C. K. ALLEN

Indecisive woolliness is the curse of much modern democratic thought.

A. D. LINDSAY

Politics is the gentle art of getting votes from the poor and campaign funds from the rich by promising to protect each from the other.
Anon.

Democracy is the recurrent suspicion that more than half of the people are right more than half of the time.
E. B. WHITE

The first of all democratic doctrines is that all men are interesting.

G. K. CHESTERTON

Democracy substitutes election by the incompetent many for appointment by the corrupt few.
GEORGE BERNARD SHAW

The welfare of the common man is more deeply affected by the administrator than by the legislator.

STANLEY BALDWIN

Sir Winston Churchill, asked what were the qualifications essential for a politician, replied:
'The ability to foretell what will happen tomorrow, next month and next year—and to explain afterwards why it didn't happen.'

*   *   *

I do not believe in the collective wisdom of individual ignorance.

THOMAS CARLYLE

Everyone is in motion, some in quest of power, others of gain. In this universal tumult, this incessant conflict of jarring interests, this continual striving of men after fortune, where is that calm to be found that is necessary for the deeper combination of the intellect?

DE TOCQUEVILLE

While making a speech, a candidate for political office sought to discover the denominational sympathies of his audience. 'My great-grandfather,' he began, 'was an Episcopalian (stony silence), but my great-grandmother belonged to the Congregational Church (continued silence). My grandfather was a Baptist (more silence), but my grandmother was a Presbyterian (still frigid silence). But I had a great-aunt who was a Methodist (loud applause). And I have always followed my great-aunt (loud and continued cheering'). He was elected.

*   *   *

'He doesn't carry much ice,' said the late Mr. J. H. Thomas of a member who had criticized him in the house.

141

'No,' said Edward Marsh, 'and he doesn't cut many guns, either.' CHRISTOPHER HASSALL

'. . . And what we've got to do is to get right down to rock bottom, and find out where we stand, and get behind ourselves and push ourselves along . . .'
MILTON HAYES

I do not believe that you can make a razor blade sharp by Act of Parliament.
MR JOHN RODGERS, MP

On one occasion, in the Ladies' Gallery, I remember the old Lady Londonderry using such language about a Liberal speaker, whose timid wife sat cowering a few feet off, that I protested and sent down a note of complaint to the Speaker of the day—Mr Lowther. He sent me back a note in reply:

'Dear Miss Asquith,
        I am so sorry but I am too busy at the moment coping with the devils below to be able to deal with the angels above.'
LADY VIOLET BONHAM-CARTER

If it were not for the Government, we should have nothing left to laugh at in France.
NICHOLAS CHAMFORT (1741-94)

The antics of our governments, national and local during the last twenty years have struck me as a series of attempts to legislate for crises—and no man ever did regulate a crisis that way.
E. HORSFALL TURNER

I don't make jokes: I just watch the government and report the facts.

*   *   *

The perfect civil servant: a man who can think of a valid objection to any possible solution.

*   *   *

Mr Speaker, I do not, more than another man, mind being cheated at cards, but I find it a little nauseating, if my opponent then publicly ascribes his success to the partnership of the Most High!

F. E. SMITH, MP
(later the 1st Earl of Birkenhead, in his maiden
speech in the House of Commons)

Intended to allay the violence of party spirit:
   God Bless the King! I mean the Faith's Defender;
   God bless—no harm in blessing—the Pretender!
   But who Pretender is, or who is King,
   God bless us all!—that's quite another thing.

JOHN BYROM

When the politicians complain that TV turns their proceedings into a circus, it should be made clear that the circus was already there, and that TV has merely demonstrated that not all the performers are well trained.

MR ED. MURROW

PRAYERS AND SERMONS

*

None preaches better than the ant, and she says nothing.

BENJAMIN FRANKLIN

A poor Scottish woman was asked if she ever attended the church of the late Dr Chalmers, once a famous Scottish preacher and divine.

'Ou ay,' she replied, 'there's a man called Chalmers preaches there, and I whiles gang in and hear him, just to encourage him, puir body!' DEAN RAMSAY

* * *

A Baptist minister named David Dewar was elected a member of the Prison Board in Scotland and called upon to give his vote in the choice of a Chaplain from the licentiates of the Established Kirk. The candidate who had gained the confidence of the Board had proved rather an indifferent preacher in a charge to which he had previously been appointed; and on David being asked to signify his assent to the choice of the Board, he said: 'Well, I've no objections to the man, for I understand he has preached a Kirk toom (empty) already, and if he be as successful in the jail, he'll maybe preach it vawcant as weel.'

ibid

* * *

In the Victorian era many nonconformist preachers used to make long extempore prayers from the pulpit, and, as has been said, some of them, 'grew garrulous with God'.

At the first service held in a newly-built church somewhere in the Midlands one Minister opened his prayers thus:

'O Lord, Thou seest us gathered here together in what must be one of the finest architectural buildings in the north of England.'

Another minister began an extempore prayer by saying: 'Paradoxical though it may seem to Thee, O Lord . . .'

There is, too, the well-known story of the Scottish minister. After several weeks of drought the local crops were threatened by days of incessant rain. 'O Lord,' said the minister, 'we know that a few weeks ago we prayed for rain; but, O Lord, *do be reasonable*!'

*   *   *

There is the story, too, of the visiting nonconformist minister who concluded his sermon with this piece of high-flown oratory:

'As I came away from the platform of your station yesterday I was stopped by a man. He did not ask me whence I had come; he did not ask me where I was going. All he said to me was: *"Tickets, please!"* And so, my friends, it will be with us when we reach the end of the long journey which we call Life. We shall not be asked whence we have come; we shall not be asked where we are going. All that will be said to us is: *"Have you got the blood-red ticket of the Lamb?"* '

*   *   *

'Have you been to Church, Tommy?'
'Yes.'
'What was the sermon about?'
'Sin.'
'What did the parson say about it?'
'He was agin it.'

*   *   *

Dr Norman Macleod was on a Highland loch when a storm came on which threatened serious consequences. The doctor, a large powerful man, was accompanied by a clerical friend of diminutive size, who began to speak seriously to the boatman of their danger, and proposed that all present should join in prayer.

'Na, na,' said the chief boatman, 'let the *little* ane gang to pray, but first the big ane maun tak that oar.'

DEAN RAMSAY

Sir, a woman's preaching is like a dog's walking on his hinder legs. It is not done well; but you are surprised to find it done at all.

DR JOHNSON

Vicar (announcing his text): ' "How long, O Lord?"— observe the pregnant aposiopesis!'

*   *   *

Gradation in Graces:

A nonconformist minister used to go as a visiting preacher to various churches in his district and was invited to a mid-day Sunday dinner by some prominent member of the congregation. He appreciated good food, and he is reputed to have a whole series of 'graces', appropriate to the meals which were placed before him. If it were a meagre repast he would use the grace: 'For these, the least of all Thy mercies, we offer our humble and grateful thanks.' If, on the other hand, he saw viands of which he was particularly fond, he would resort to a long grace which began: 'O most bountiful Jehovah.'

*   *   *

'O Lord, I am only a humble worm blowing the gospel trumpet.'

*   *   *

'Well, at least she needn't say the Weaver's Prayer.'
'What's that?'
'The Weaver's Prayer?—"O Lord, keep us in good conceit of ourselves." '

*　　*　　*

An evangelist, who preached a fiery gospel, invited questions from his 'open-air' audience. A sarcastic listener promptly said : 'What's worrying me is how am I going to get a shirt on over my wings when I die?'

'Don't you worry, my friend,' replied the evangelist. 'Your trouble will be getting your trousers on over your tail.'

The Dalesman

A local preacher substituting for a minister was approaching the house where he was to have tea in the village of W——, when he heard a voice call, 'You can put t'ham away, it's only t' local.'

ibid.

An old man at Heptonstall told the young local preacher at the conclusion of his service, 'Tha sings like tha preaches —baht notes.'

ibid.

There is, perhaps, no greater hardship at present inflicted on mankind in civilized and free countries, than the necessity of listening to someone.

ANTHONY TROLLOPE

' 'As 'e done yet?' a rather deaf member of the congregation whispered to his neighbour, referring to a long-winded preacher.

' 'E's done long ago,' his neighbour replied—'but 'e won't gi' o'er!'

*　　*　　*

A young minister just out of college asked his uncle, a Scottish elder,

'Weel, Uncle, an' what did ye think o' ma sermon?'

'Sin' ye ask it, laddie, I *didna* like it—and for three reasons. First, ye read it. Second, ye read it badly. And third, it were no' worth reading.'

* * *

Earnest negro convert to pastor:

'Yes, boss, I prays the Almighty every day to use ma services, if only in an advisory capacity.'

* * *

Welsh minister (in an opening prayer before a lecture by Mr Bernard Newman):

'Oh, Lord, bless our speaker tonight, Mr Newman, whom Thou doubtless knowest . . .'

PROGRESS

*

What we call 'Progress' is the exchange of one nuisance for another nuisance.

HAVELOCK ELLIS

Technological progress has merely provided us with more efficient means for going backwards.

ALDOUS HUXLEY

True progress quietly and persistently moves along without notice.

ST FRANCIS DE SALES

I have always considered that the substitution of the internal combustion engine for the horse marked a very gloomy milestone in the progress of mankind.

SIR WINSTON CHURCHILL

George Stephenson met with both opposition and ridicule when he was working on the invention of the railroad engine. 'Carriage makers and coachmen will starve for want of work,' it was said. .

A House of Commons Committee asked Stephenson: 'If a cow gets on the track of the engine travelling ten miles an hour, will it not be an awkward situation?'

'Yes, very awkward, indeed—for the cow,' replied Stephenson.

PUNS

*

A small boy asked his mother: 'Do you know what makes the Tower of Pisa lean?'
And she said: 'No, if I did, I would take some.'

*   *   *

May my last breath be drawn through a pipe and exhaled in a pun.

CHARLES LAMB

Asked by his girl friend: 'What *is* euphoria?'' an inveterate punster made one of the worst puns of all time: 'Eu for me, and me for eu!'

*   *   *

After the Convention under which the French evacuated Portugal in 1808 (negotiated by Sir Hew Dalrymple) Canning blandly announced that he should in future spell humiliation with a 'Hew'!

*   *   *

Accompanied by a huge St Bernard dog a Knight walked through wind and snow. At last, late at night, he came to a castle and knocked at the door.
'No one can enter here,' said a gruff voice.
'But,' said the Knight, 'surely you would not send a knight out on a dog like this.'

*   *   *

A Vintage Limerick:

> There was an old man of Boulong
> Who *would* sing a topical song.
> It wasn't the words
> That frightened the birds
> But the horrible *double entong*.

*   *   *

Punning is a talent that no man affects to despise but he that is without it.

JONATHAN SWIFT

The audience strummed their catarrhs.

ALEXANDER WOOLLCOTT

'Doctor, I've got Bright's disease, and he's got mine.'

S. J. PERELMAN

RADIO

*

Some of the performers who've become teen-age institutions sound as though they belong in one.

PAUL HARTMAN

The ideal voice for radio may be defined as having no substance, no sex, no owner, and a message of importance to every housewife.

HARRY V. WADE

Sense doesn't make sense in radio.

FRED ALLEN

Two men were discussing the merits of their respective wireless sets.

'Has your set good receptivity?' one asked.

'I'll say it has,' the other replied. 'I was listening to a quartet the other night, and I didn't like the tenor, so I tuned him out and listened to the other three.'

*   *   *

So here's to the radio speaker,
Let him rave and rant and scoff;
If we do not like the things he says
We can always turn him off.

Anon.

Next to radio, the greatest boon to mankind is undoubtedly the knob which switches it off.

Anon.

I would not trust some members of the Brains Trust

with the education of a tom-tit, much less a human being.

CANON A. L. KEITH

The young man reading the love lyric makes a noise like the mating of dinosaurs.

STEPHEN POTTER

There are indications that the BBC is about to try the experiment of giving listeners what they themselves think they think they want, instead of what the BBC thinks they think they think they want.

Punch

RELATIONS

*

Distant relatives are the best kind, and the further the better.

F. M. HUBBARD

Visit your aunt, but not every day; and call at your brother's, but not every night.

BENJAMIN FRANKLIN

I advise thee to visit thy relations and friends; but I advise thee not to live too near them.

DR. THOMAS FULLER

Don't despise your poor relatives; they may become suddenly rich some day.

JOSH BILLINGS

Relations are simply a tedious pack of people who haven't got the remotest knowledge of how to live nor the smallest instinct about how to die.

OSCAR WILDE

RELIGION

*

A religion that is small enough for our understanding would not be large enough for our needs.

A. J. BALFOUR

Immortality is the genius to move others long after you yourself have stopped moving.

FRANK ROONEY

All the different religions are only so many religious dialects.

G. C. LICHTENBERG

A gentle Quaker, hearing a strange noise in his house one night, got up and discovered a burglar busily at work, so he went and got his gun, then came back and stood quietly in the doorway.

'Friend,' he said, 'I would do thee no harm for the world, but thou standest where I am about to shoot.'

REPARTEE

*

Here lies our sovereign Lord the King,
    Whose word no man relies on,
Who never said a foolish thing,
    Nor ever did a wise one.

(THE EARL OF ROCHESTER's quatrain on King Charles II.
The King retorted: 'My words are my own but my acts are
my ministers'.')

*   *   *

Ignorance, Madam, pure ignorance.
(DR JOHNSON's reply to a lady who inquired why he had
given an inaccurate definition of the word *pastern* in the
Dictionary.)

*   *   *

Repartee is something we think of twenty-four hours
too late.

MARK TWAIN

When advised by his doctor to take a walk on an empty
stomach, Sydney Smith inquired: 'Whose?'

*   *   *

'I never saw sunsets like yours, Mr Turner,' said a lady
to the famous artist.
'Don't you wish you did?' he replied.

*   *   *

A director, who imagined himself to be something of a 'lady-killer', was asking an applicant about her secretarial qualifications.

'Yes,' she said, 'my typing's pretty accurate. I know *your* type for a start.'

* * *

Dr Charles Hill, MP, Chancellor of the Duchy of Lancaster, was speaking at a political meeting.

'The death rate has gone down,' he said, 'and the infant death rate has gone down.'

'Aye, and t'birth rate's gone down, too!' said a heckler in the audience.

'Well,' said Dr Hill, 'if you had only stayed at home instead of interrupting political meetings . . .'

* * *

When Shaw was making his 'curtain speech at the end of a first night of one of his plays, a man in the gallery shouted: 'Boo'.

'I certainly agree with you, my dear sir,' said GBS. '—but what are we two against so many?'

* * *

'No, Stella, I will *not* play horse to your Lady Godiva!'

(GEORGE BERNARD SHAW to Mrs Patrick Campbell, when she wanted to publish all his letters to her while he was alive.')

* * *

When a lady told Thomas Carlyle that she accepted the universe, he said: 'My God, madam, you'd better!'

* * *

SCIENCE

*

I would rather discover one scientific fact than become King of Persia.

DEMOCRITUS

Every branch of science has an *argot* of its own, and even physicists often use ordinary language like the rest of us.

STUART CLOSE

Increasingly and of necessity the brilliant scientist in one subject is a layman in another. The task of being a master in his own subject exhausts his capacities.

GERALD HEARD

It was Einstein who made the real trouble. He announced in 1905 that there was no such thing as absolute rest. After that there never was.

STEPHEN LEACOCK

Apparently a scientist is a man who surveys all the sciences without any particular study of them, and then gives expression to his own moral principles or prejudices.

G. K. CHESTERTON

Nature, and Nature's laws, lay hid in night;
God said : *Let Newton be!* and all was light.

ALEXANDER POPE

It did not last : the Devil, howling *Ho!*
Let Einstein be! restored the status quo.

SIR JOHN SQUIRE

Science is always wrong: it never solves a problem without creating ten more.

GEORGE BERNARD SHAW

In everything that relates to science, I am a whole encyclopaedia behind the rest of the world.

CHARLES LAMB

Scientists are men who prolong life so that we can have time to pay for their inventions.   *Anon.*

There is a great deal of life which science does not cover; from which indeed it explicitly dissociates itself. Science is limited to describing the structure of things. Science can analyse the alternations of sound and silence that go to make up a piece of music, but it is quite powerless to explain why one piece is an immortal masterpiece and another in similar form is ephemeral rubbish. Science can analyse the chemical components and anatomical proportions of a human being, but give no qualitative account of his personality. Eddington, Whitehead, Jeans, Sullivan and many another have made this point, if only in order to defend science from the charge of failing to do something which it has never claimed to do, and never will.

L. A. G. STRONG

Scientific controversies constantly resolve themselves into differences about the meaning of words.

PROFESSOR A. SCHUSTER

Comforting News About Strontium 90
(or Who will Debunk the Debunkers?)

Conclusions of Professor Mayneord, Professor of Physics in the British Post-Graduate Medical Federation, about the hazard to man of nuclear and allied radiation.
A typical high-carbohydrate British dirt contains amounts of radium and thorium equivalent in their effect to some

300 times the present intake of strontium 90 from nuclear explosions. The amounts of radium and thorium eaten by three or four members of a single family could vary by several times or even a thousand times according to their individual tastes in food; and most of the radioactive material that goes into the body comes out again within 48 hours.

Four ounces of Brazil nuts contain three times as much radium and thorium as the entire bone and soft tissue of a normal adult. An anti-nausea preparation for pregnant women contains 50,000 times as much radio-active material as the present intake of strontium 90 from food. The soft tissues of the body, which in the past have been ignored, contribute one-quarter of the body's total content of radium and thorium; and herbiverous animals, headed by Welsh sheep and Sahara camels, have up to 60 times as much in their bones as man.

* * *

Jack : 'Yes, but you said yourself that a severe chill was not hereditary.'

Algernon : 'It usen't to be, I know—but I daresay it is now. Science is always making wonderful improvements in things.'

OSCAR WILDE

During a recent convention of atom scientists at Las Vegas, one of the Professors spent all his free time at the gambling tables. Two colleagues were discussing their friend's weakness.

'Hotchkiss gambles as if there were no tomorrow,' said one.

'Perhaps,' commented the other, 'he *knows* something!'

* * *

I could wish that in the next era of 'civilization' the monkeys may get on top and begin shooting scientists into space.

REV. J. E. E. TUNSTALL

The inference we can draw from an analytical study of the difference between ourselves and other animals is surely this: that the bells which toll for mankind are—most of them, anyway—like the bells on Alpine cattle; they are attached to our own necks, and it must be *our* fault if they do not make a cheerful and harmonious sound.

P. B. MEDAWAR, FRS

As soon as a human invention is complete and taken up internationally, the only remaining constructive approach is to learn how to live with it and, above all, how to control it.

DAVID WALKER

If the Russians get to Venus they will find it boiling hot. If they get to Mars they will find it freezing cold. On neither planet will they be able to breathe. The best of luck to them.

THE ASTRONOMER ROYAL

Does not the moon shine in the heaven to warn us that our proud civilization is under the universal doom of death? So much science can predict. But no science can predict the *manner of dying*. Mankind will certainly perish, but not necessarily like the brutes.

L. P. JACKS

*

It is an inflexible rule of mine not to make impromptu speeches without good warning . . . As Lord Goddard said, they are not worth the paper they are written on.

E. HORSFALL TURNER

A dinner-table is the only place where one is not bored —for the first hour.

MAX O'RELL

'It is most unfortunate that he can't be here. I am sure that, if he were, he would be the first to apologise for his absence.'

*   *   *

'This occasion gives me an opportunity to shake hands with many old faces.'

*   *   *

'It may help you,' Mark Twain once said to an obviously nervous guest of honour at a dinner, 'if you keep one thing in mind. Just remember that *they don't expect much!*'

*   *   *

That man—he'd talk a spider to death!

LINCOLNSHIRE SAYING

It was the annual meeting of an East Yorkshire organization, and the chairman was making his yearly speech.

'In most similar societies,' he said, 'half the committee

does all the work, while the other half does nothing. I am
pleased to place on record that in the society over which
I have the honour to preside it is just the reverse.'

The Dalesman

(A few mayoral *obiter dicta*)
'I am deeply sensible of the honour you have done by
electing me to be first citizen of the borough, and I shall
try during my year of office to hold evenly the scales of
justice, veering neither to partiality on the one hand nor to
impartiality on the other.'

*   *   *

'I know that a Mayor should be, like Caesar's wife, all
things to all men.'

*   *   *

'Aldermen and Councillors, the rates in this borough are
creeping up by leaps and bounds.'

*   *   *

'Gentlemen, I am taking upon myself the morality for
the first time, and I expect that the duties will be very
onious.'

STATISTICS

*

The Deputation produced the most elaborate figures to prove that so dense was the population that a railway line through the overcrowded area would earn immense profits, and would turn the whole of that part of Mayo into the wealthiest part of the British Isles. Duke* heard them through, and then, with his extraordinary memory, told the Deputation that, only a few years previously, a deputation had waited on the then Chief Secretary to ask for a grant in aid of poor relief in the district, and that on that occasion they had produced figures to show that the population was so small, with so little resources and so little trade that they were all on the brink of starvation . . .

The Chairman of the Deputation looked at Duke in amazement. Was the Chief Secretary going mad, or what, he wondered.

'Sure, man alive,' he said to him, 'them figures were for an entirely and taytotally different purpose!' He told Mick afterwards that 'he'd often heard tell of the quare ways of the English, but begad, when you get wan of them who expects you to prove the population big with precisely the same figures as you used on an entirely different occasion to prove it was small, well what could mortal man do with them?'

SIR CHRISTOPHER LYNCH-ROBINSON, BART.

He uses statistics as a drunken man uses lamp-posts—for support rather than for illumination.

ANDREW LANG

* The Chief Secretary for Ireland.

Statistics are like alienists—they will testify for either side.

F. H. LA GUARDIA

Statistician—A man who can go directly from an unwarranted assumption to a preconceived conclusion.

*

A native African chieftain had a gold throne of which he was very proud. When war broke out with a neighbouring tribe he ordered that the gold throne should be hidden in the roof of his grass hut. But his enemies were victorious in the ensuing battle, sacked his village and set fire to his hut, and in due course the gold throne was found and pillaged.

And the moral of the story is that those who live in grass houses should not stow thrones.

* * *

A man and a woman were the only passengers in a 'non-smoking' railway carriage. The lady had a small lap-dog which she lifted on to the seat beside her.

After the train had started the man filled his pipe and lit it.

'This is a non-smoking compartment,' said the woman, 'and I object to smoking.'

'And I,' said the man, rudely, 'object to animals sitting on railway carriage seats. The floor is the proper place for them.'

This reply so infuriated the woman traveller that she seized the man's pipe and threw it out of the window. With equal suddenness the man seized the lap-dog and threw it after the pipe.

The woman pulled the communication cord. The train stopped. Both climbed out on to the permanent way and began to put their respective complaints to the guard—when their argument and altercation came to an abrupt end through the arrival of the little dog, which trotted up, wagging its tail—*with the pipe in its mouth!*

* * *

Two old men were sitting deep in armchairs in the reading room of a London club. One of them noticed that every few minutes his companion emitted a deep chuckle; or sometimes, as an alternative, he made a quick, deprecating gesture with his right hand, as if he were dismissing or disparaging something.

'Excuse me, sir,' said the observer, 'but would you tell me what you find so amusing in this rather sepulchral room?'

'Not at all,' replied the other—'I'm telling myself funny stories.'

'And when you don't laugh—but make that funny little gesture?'

'Oh, *that*. That's when I've heard it before!'

*   *   *

A man had been condemned to death by an Oriental King, but was granted a reprieve when he undertook that, if he were allowed to live, he would teach the King's ass to speak within a year.

'How could you promise so foolish a thing?' asked some of his friends, when they heard of the undertaking.

'Nay, it is no foolish thing,' the man replied. 'For, within a year, the King may die, or *I* may die, or the *ass* may die—or the ass may speak!'

*   *   *

A young husband and his wife were watching a television programme one evening, when the screen suddenly went black. They could not understand why, until the mystery was solved by their poodle. He came up to them with the flex plug in his mouth, dropped it in front of them, blinked, and remarked: 'Now isn't it time for that perishing walk?'

*   *   *

TIME

*

I have a special vocabulary of my own: I 'pass away time' when it is ill or uneasy, but when 'tis good I do not pass it away: I taste it over again and adhere to it; one must run over the ill and settle upon the good.

MONTAIGNE

A moment in time but time was made through that moment; for without the meaning there is no time, and that moment of time gave the meaning.

T. S. ELIOT

As if you could kill time without injuring eternity!

THOREAU

He was always late on principle, his principle being that punctuality is the thief of time.

OSCAR WILDE

You are not born to fame if you do not know the value of time.

VAAVENARGUES

Nothing puzzles me more than time and space, and yet nothing puzzles me less, for I never think about them.

CHARLES LAMB

Haut et bas, gauche et droite,
Avenirs et passés,
Sont dans la même boîte
L'un sur l'autre entassés.

JEAN COCTEAU

TOWN AND COUNTRY

*

I read of mornings the same old books over and over again, having no command of new ones; walk with my great black dog of an afternoon, and at evening sit with open windows, up to which China roses climb, with my pipe, while the blackbirds and thrushes begin to rustle bedwards in the garden, and the nightingale to have the neighbourhood to herself.

EDWARD FITZGERALD

You think I live in Epicurean ease; but this happens to be a jolly day; one isn't always well or tolerably good, the weather is not always clear, nor nightingales singing, nor Tacitus full of pleasant atrocity. But such as life is, I believe I have got hold of a good end of it.

ibid

I have no relish for the country; it is a kind of healthy grave.

SYDNEY SMITH

We have a maiden aunt in our family, and the legend is that some years ago she decided, after forty years of city life, to retire and start a poultry farm. She bought a house in the country with some land and huts close by. Then she went off to acquire her stock of poultry. She came back quite pleased with herself, having ordered sixty hens and sixty roosters.

*   *   *

'During the war my husband sent our new land-girl out with a horse and cart to collect some turnips. 'He's a quiet horse,' said my husband, 'if the rein doesn't touch his back.'

At dinner time she was back and we asked how she had fared. 'Oh, we'd one or two showers,' said the girl, 'but I kept the rain off him with my mac.'

The Dalesman

* * *

The d——d smutty atmosphere clings to you like a wet blanket.

EDWARD FITZGERALD
(of London)

I know nothing for which this town is remarkable, except for being very populous and very poor.

DANIEL DEFOE
(of Sudbury)

Battles have been fought, kings have died, history has transacted itself; but, all unheeding and untouched, Dream-thorp has watched apple-trees redden, and wheat ripen, and smoked its pipe, and quaffed its mug of beer, and rejoiced over its new-born children, and with proper solemnity carried its dead to the churchyard.

ALEXANDER SMITH

Surely one of the best ways to satisfy one's love of one's country is to plant trees and thus leave a living memorial.

RICHARD ST BARBE BAKER

An agricultural lecturer in Yorkshire was addressing a gathering of farmers at a demonstration which sought to show modern development in manuring. He put his hand in his right waistcoat pocket, drew it out, and opened it in what he thought was a dramatic manner.

'Some day,' he said, 'in the palm of my hand you will be able to hold enough manure to manure one acre. Just think of it!'

An elderly farmer at the back of the room spoke up. 'Aye, 'appen,' he said. ' 'Appen it will—but t'crops tha gets off it'll go into t'other waistcoat pocket.'

The Dalesman

TOBACCO

*

I kissed my first woman and smoked my first cigarette on the same day; I have never had time for tobacco since.

ARTURO TOSCANINI

Tobacco has been my evening comfort and my morning curse.

CHARLES LAMB

Perfection is such a nuisance that I often regret having cured myself of using tobacco.

ÉMILE ZOLA

John liked his pipe, but the parson disapproved of smoking and made this plain every time he met John. Invariably he stopped and took John to task in the usual vein. 'John,' he confronted John one morning. 'If the Lord had intended you to smoke, He'd have put a chimney in the top of your head.'

'Aye,' retaliated John, 'and if He'd meant thoo ta tak' snuff, He'd ah put thi noase t'other way up.'

*   *   *

TRANQUILLITY

*

Nothing contributes more to peace of mind than to have no opinions whatever.

G. C. LICHTENBERG

Periods of tranquillity are seldom prolific of creative achievement. Mankind has to be stirred up.

ALFRED NORTH WHITEHEAD

It is difficult to keep quiet if you have nothing to do.

SCHOPENHAUER

Blessed are they who have nothing to say, and who cannot be persuaded to say it.

*   *   *

TRAVEL

*

The only way of catching a train I ever discovered is to miss the train before.

G. K. CHESTERTON

Surely to have seen Athens gives a man what Swift calls Invisible Precedence over his fellows.

SIR EDWARD MARSH

At the Customs sheds a returning traveller was asked if he had any pornographic literature in his luggage.

'Certainly not,' he said indignantly. 'I don't even own a pornograph!'

* * *

Travel may broaden the mind, but it certainly depletes the purse.

* * *

I would rather have a third-class ticket round my brain than a first-class ticket round the world.

FRANK HARRIS

Foreign travel today has become simply a question of 'Keeping up with the Joneses'.

* * *

The globe-trotter lives in a smaller world than the peasant.

G. K. CHESTERTON

Mirabell: For travel! Why, the man that I mean is above forty.

Fairall: No matter for that; 'tis for the honour of England, that all Europe should know we have blockheads of all ages.

WILLIAM CONGREVE

First Bull-fight
'. . . in Valencia, when sweet young Spanish girls looked on with perfect pleasure, and Delia shouted: "Go on, bull." '

Extract from a letter

VERSATILITY

*

I, Richard Furness, schoolmaster, Don,
Keep parish books and pay the poor,
Draw plans for buildings and indite,
Letters for those who cannot write;
Make wills and recommend a proctor,
Cure wounds, let blood with any doctor,
Draw teeth, sing songs, the hautboy play
At chapel on each hold day,
Paint sign-boards, cart-names at command,
Survey and plot estates of land,
Collect at Easter one in ten
And on the Sunday say 'Amen'.

RICHARD FURNESS (circa 1832)

WAR

*

'I do greatly suspect that all this enterprise will be like the tale of the pitcher full of milk wherewith a shoemaker made himself rich in conceit; but when the pitcher was broken, he had not whereupon to dine . . . What do you pretend by these large conquests? You will only break your pitcher.'

'Oh,' said Count Swashbuckle, 'here is a fine simpleton! Come, let us hide ourselves in the corner of a chimney, and thus spend our life among the ladies, knitting and spinning and threading pearls. He that nothing ventures finds neither horse nor mule.'

'But he who ventures too much,' rejoined Mr Sobersense, 'loses both horse and mule.'

FRANÇOIS RABELAIS

We must all have learnt, even the tyrants, that in another total war—with or without unleashing all the demons locked in the atom—there can be no victors, only survivors.

ADLAI E. STEVENSON

The humanizing of war! You might as well talk of humanizing Hell!

LORD FISHER

WEATHER

*

I once met an old man on a lonely road over a bog in the County Kerry. It was a warm, bright midsummer's day under a cloudless sky, and the old fellow had slipped the creel of turf off his back to sit down by the side of the road to rest.

'It's a fine day,' said I.

'Aye,' he replied in his soft Kerry speech, 'it is so. A body would be contint, if he had time, to go on his way and to come back.'

SIR CHRISTOPHER LYNCH-ROBINSON

'Is that God?' a small boy asked his mother on hearing the weather forecast on the radio.

'Why should you think that?' said his mother.

'Well,' he replied, 'who else would know what the weather's going to do?'

Happy New Year (1779)

Jan. 1. Storm all night. The may-pole is blown down. Thatch and tiles damaged. Great damage is done both by sea and land.

Jan. 4. Water froze in my chamber-window.

Jan. 10. My therm is broken.

Jan. 16. Sowed the great mead in part, and all Berriman's field (laid down last year with grass-seeds) with good peat ashes.

Jan. 17. Ice on ponds is very thick.

Jan. 22. Bees come out, and gather on the snowdrops. Many gnats in the air.

Jan. 29. Out of the wind there is frost, but none where the S. wind blows.

Jan. 30. Tulips begin to peep.

Feb. 7. Lambs come very fast. Bats appear. Field- are sowing.

Feb. 9. The garden works well: sowed peas and planted beans. Crocuses blow.

GILBERT WHITE

Everybody talks about the weather, but nobody does anything about it.

CHARLES DUDLEY WARREN

A Polish boy rushed in and said excitedly to his mother: 'We've been taken over by Russia.'

'That is nice,' she said. 'Now we won't have to endure those cold Polish winters!'

*   *   *

If you don't like the weather in New England, just wait a few minutes.

MARK TWAIN

A village woman was complaining about fog to a rather 'arty-crafty' acquaintance.

'It's not fog,' said the latter. 'It's wonderful ozone from the sea. You should breathe it in.'

'Yew call it wot yew loike,' said the country-woman— 'I calls it FOG!'

WIT AND HUMOUR

*

A man may enjoy humour all by himself; he may see a joke when no one else sees it; he may see the point and avoid it.

But wit is a sword; it is meant to make people feel the point as well as see it. All honest people saw the point of Mark Twain's wit. Not a few dishonest people felt it.

G. K. CHESTERTON

Individuals will laugh at a joke they do not see because others who see it do.

SOMERSET MAUGHAM

Men show their character in nothing more clearly than by what they find laughable.

GOETHE

There are only three basic jokes, but since the mother-in-law joke is not a joke but a very serious question, there are only two.

GEORGE ADE

Anything is funny, provided that it doesn't happen to *us*.
Anon.

You may know many things about humour; you may use it with deadly or uproarious effect; you may enjoy it or earn your bread with it; you may classify it and discover penetrating truths about it. But you still do not know what it is.

GEORGE MIKES

Humour is consistent with pathos, whilst wit is not.

SAMUEL TAYLOR COLERIDGE

A very little wit is valued in a woman, as we are pleased with a few words spoken plain by a parrot.

JONATHAN SWIFT

Wit is the sudden marriage of ideas which before their marriage were not perceived to have any relation.

MARK TWAIN

Wit consists in knowing the resemblance of things that differ and the difference of things that are alike.

MADAME DE STAIL

Wit is a form of lightning calculation; humour the exploitation of disproportion.

RUSSELL GREEN

WORDS

*

Words are not merely the vehicles in which thought is delivered; they are part of thinking.

P. B. MEDAWAR

Flowery language is permissible only when the flowers are perfectly fresh.

Anon.

The pleasure and excitement of words is that they are living and generating things.

CHRISTOPHER FRY

I love rare, incomprehensible words.

MAXIM GORKY

There is only one rule for being a good talker: learn to listen.

CHRISTOPHER MORLEY

I once knew a fellow who spoke a dialect with an accent.

IRVIN S. COBB

The art of writing is the art of applying the seat of the pants to the seat of the chair.

MARY HEATON VOSSE

Similes
Motionless as a King's mummy in a catacomb.

FLAUBERT

The quarrels of lovers are like summer showers, that leave the country more verdant and beautiful.

MADAME NICKIN

Passive as a tabby-cat.

Anon.

Laugh, like parrots, at a bag-piper.
SHAKESPEARE

Laughed like a bowlful of jelly.
C. C. MOORE

*   *   *

Sydney Smith once saw a child stroking a tortoise. 'This,' he said, 'is like scratching the dome of St Paul's to please the Dean and Chapter!'

*   *   *

'You all know, neighbours, what a man I be, and how I come down with my powerful words when my pride is boiling wi' scorn.'

THOMAS HARDY

Even the weariest river
Winds somewhere safe to sea.
A. C. SWINBURNE

The debates of today are not, as the wrangles of the Middle Ages, the battles of brain against brain, but a duet of defiances hurled from behind the fortification, a banging of the big drum and a deciding of the issue in favour of the bigger din.

FRANK BINDER

We have to make use of language, which is made up necessarily of pre-conceived ideas. Such ideas unconsciously held are the most dangerous of all.

RAYMOND POINCARÉ

Officialese (from a letter to *The Times*)

'I had occasion some time since to ask a Government Department to supply me with a book for official use. I was informed in reply that, although the Department was not in a position to meet my request, I was "authorized to acquire the work in question through the ordinary trade channels. Or, as we should say, "buy it."

It would be easy to add to Mr Herbert's list of words which mark the tendency he deplores. "Assist" for "help", "endeavour" for "try", "proceed" for "go", "purchase" for "buy", "approximately" for "about", "sufficient" for "enough", "attired" for "dressed", "inquire" for "ask", are general in speech as well as print.'

*   *   *

Vogue Words
Blue-print is one of those vogue words which have been spawned by officialdom and journalism acting in unholy conjunction.

ERIC PARTRIDGE

Have you noticed that, in newspaper leaders today, nothing ever 'comes' or 'rises' or 'springs' from anything else? It always 'stems'.

*   *   *

Churchilliana
(1) Eating words has never given me indigestion.

(2) A Minister, in his efforts to avoid ending a sentence with a preposition, had produced an extremely complicated and pompous minute.

Churchill scribbled on it the following comment: 'This is an example of bastard and stilted English, *up with which I will not put*. WSC.'

(3) A minute which Sir Winston wrote on another memorandum submitted to him was: 'This appears to in-

clude every cliché known to the English language except "Please adjust your dress before leaving." WSC.'

*   *   *

LITERARISMS are the journalese of the literary, or such unusual words as are used only by the literary or the learned. Examples are:

alembicated	dichotomy	nepenthe
autocthonous	epicene	significant
cathartic	etiolated	viable
crepuscular	ineluctable	wilderness

ERIC PARTRIDGE

A prose style may often be improved by striking out every other word from each sentence when written.

SYDNEY SMITH

For in truth all art does but consist in the removal of surplusage.

WALTER PATER

*   *   *

Scientists' Vocabulary

Phrase	*Meaning*
It has long been known that	I haven't bothered to look up the original reference
......of great theoretical and practical importance	.........interesting to me
......accidentally stained during mounting	dropped on the floor
It is suggested that............	I think.........
It is believed that............	
It may be that...............	
It is clear that much additional work will be required before a complete understanding	I don't understand it

Unfortunately, a quantitative theory to account for these effects has not been formulated	Neither does anybody else
Correct within an order of magnitude	.........wrong

*　　　*　　　*

In 1814 the Duke of Wellington, returned to England after the Peninsula War, was entertained to dinner by the Prince Regent, who proposed his health. The Duke rose, smiling broadly, and began :

'I want words to express . . .'

The Regent promptly interrupted him with royal geniality.

'My dear fellow,' said Prinny, in his easy way, 'we know your *actions*, and we will excuse you your words, so sit down.'

The Duke, always obedient to royalty, sat down 'with all the delight of a schoolboy who has been given an unexpected holiday.'

PHILIP GUEDALLA

All good writing is *swimming under water* and holding your breath.

SCOTT FITZGERALD

There is a great discovery still to be made in literature, that of paying literary men by the quantity they do not write.

THOMAS CARLYLE

The English language is the richest in the world in monosyllables.

STANLEY BALDWIN

'When you say "hill",' the Queen interrupted, '*I* could show you hills, in comparison with which you'd call that a valley.'

'No, I shouldn't,' said Alice, surprised into contradicting her at last: 'a hill *can't* be a valley, you know. That would be nonsense—'

The Red Queen shook her head. 'You may call it "nonsense" if you like,' she said, 'but *I've* heard nonsense, compared with which that would be as sensible as a dictionary!'

LEWIS CARROLL

WORK

*

Work expands so as to fill the time available for its completion. ('Parkinson's Law'.)

C. NORTHCOTE PARKINSON

I like work; it fascinates me. I can sit and look at it for hours.

JEROME K. JEROME

Overheard: 'Well, it's an *insedative* to work!'

* * *

I do most of my work sitting down: that's where I shine.

ROBERT BUSHBY

Gilbreth carried out his original experiments on bricklaying. This, it is generally felt, was very subtle of him, because bricklayers being what they are, he clearly was not going to have much trouble in finding quicker ways to do the work. From the first he obtained marvellous results, and it was found that only the very fastest spiders could work quickly enough to spin webs on bricklayers working by Gilbreth's methods.

'MARK SPADE'

. . . that purest of human pleasures—watching other people work!

Anon.

Some temptations come to the industrious, but all temptations come to the idle.

* * *

No one who does not enjoy work can truly enjoy anything else.

*   *   *

You cannot build a reputation on things you are going to do.

*   *   *

Many receive advice but only the wise profit by it.

*   *   *

Nothing dignifies human labour as much as the saving of it.

MR JOHN RODGERS, MP

It is difficult to keep quiet if you have nothing to do.

SCHOPENHAUER

It is difficult to fool the people you work for; still more difficult to fool the people you work with; but almost impossible to fool those who work under your direction.

Efficiency Magazine

Buying and selling is good and necessary; it is very necessary, and may, possibly, be very good; but it cannot be the noblest work of man; and let us hope that in our time it may not be esteemed the noblest work of an Englishman.

ANTHONY TROLLOPE

Work is a form of nervousness.

DON HEROLD

Like every man of sense and good feeling I abominate work.

ALDOUS HUXLEY

Work is the greatest thing in the world, so we should always save some of it for tomorrow.

DON HEROLD

The good citizen does not shed his 'rights and duties' at the moment he 'knocks off' from the day's work, so as to become for the rest of the day an irresponsible amuser of himself. He takes on new rights and new duties, in some respects more interesting than those which governed his official working hours, but yet essentially of a piece with them.

L. P. JACKS

A man should live to work but not work to live.

VOLTAIRE

ACKNOWLEDGMENTS

Grateful acknowledgment is made to the following for permission to reprint quotations included in this anthology :

Mr Christopher Hassall and Messrs Longman, Green & Co Ltd for extracts from Sir Edward Marsh by Christopher Hassall;

Messrs William Heinemann Ltd for two lines from FORTY-TWO FABLES OF LA FONTAINE translated by Sir Edward Marsh;

The Earl of Birkenhead and Messrs Eyre and Spottiswoode (Publishers) Ltd for extracts from F.E. by the Earl of Birkenhead;

Olive, Lady Lynch-Robinson, for extracts from THE LAST OF THE IRISH R.M.'s by the late Sir Christopher Lynch-Robinson;

The Reader's Digest Association Ltd for extracts from The Reader's Digest, principally from the *Laughter the Best Medicine* column;

The Editor of THE DALESMAN for numerous extracts from that journal, particularly from the *Every Yorkshireman in his humour* column;

The Editor of THE SPECTATOR for a quotation from an article by Monica Furlong;

Messrs Hodder and Stoughton Ltd for an extract from THE DUKE by Philip Guedalla;

Mr Nigel Balchin and Messrs. Hamish Hamilton Ltd for extracts from HOW TO RUN A BASSOON FACTORY by Mark Spade;

Mr Stephen Potter and Messrs Rupert Hart-Davis Ltd for a quotation from SUPERMANSHIP by Stephen Potter;

Messrs Hamish Hamilton Ltd for quotations from Mr Eric Partridge and USAGE and ABUSAGE by Eric Partridge;

Lady Vansittart and Messrs Hutchinson & Co (Publishers) Ltd for quotations from THE MIST PROCESSION by Lord Vansittart;

Mr Daniel George and Hulton Bros Ltd for two extracts from A BOOK OF ANECDOTES by Daniel George;

Mrs Kathleen Hunt for several howlers from THE BEST HOWLERS and MY FAVOURITE HOWLERS by the late Mr Cecil Hunt;

Messrs Longmans, Green & Co Ltd for an extract from BY LOVE POSSESSED by J. G. Cozzens;

His Honour Judge J. Tudor Rees and Messrs Frederick Muller Ltd for extracts from RESERVED JUDGMENT by J. Tudor Rees;

Mr Russell Green and Mr Eric Horsfall Turner for some of their own unpublished epigrams; and

Mr J. B. Priestley and the Editor of the NEW STATESMAN for an extract from Mr Priestley's article 'Unsound to the Summit'.

The compiler wishes to record his especial debt of gratitude to Mr EVAN ESAR, who has kindly given him permission to include quotations from works by George Ade, Robert Benchley, Oliver Herford, H. L. Mencken, Helen Rowland and Wilson Mizner, which has already appeared in Mr Esar's A TREASURY OF WIT AND HUMOUR, the English edition of which, edited by Nicholas Bentley, is published by Phoenix House Ltd.

THE END